A ROYAL LINEAGE:

ALFRED THE GREAT.

901-1901

BY

ANNAH ROBINSON WATSON.

ISBN: 978-93-5128-795-7(HB)

First Published in 1901
Indian Reprint in 2017

Published by

Kalpaz Publications
C-30, Satyawati Nagar,
Delhi – 110052
E-mail: kalpaz@hotmail.com
Website: kalpazpublications.com
Ph.: +91-9212142040

Cataloging in Publication Data—DK
Courtesy: D.K. Agencies (P) Ltd. <docinfo@dkagencies.com>

Watson, Annah Robinson, 1848-1930, **author.**
A royal lineage : Alfred the Great, 901-1901 / by Annah Robinson Watson.
pages cm
"First published in 1901"—Title page verso.
ISBN 9789351287957

1. Alfred, King of England, 849-899—Family. 2. Families of royal descent. 3. Reed family. I. Title.

CS71.R284W38 2017 DDC 929.20942 23

Commendation from Prof. Lyon Gardiner Tyler, of William and Mary College.

I have read this valuable book, and cordially commend it for its general interest and accuracy, for the scope which it presents, its literary merit, and the skill with which the subject is handled. It is the work of a careful and conscientious writer, who has won recognition in other departments of literary endeavor, and who in this volume has succeeded in presenting in condensed form the result of much painstaking study. The royal line herein traced is undoubtedly historic, and it ought to be an inspiration to many people in our country to learn that some of the blood of the illustrious King Alfred courses through their veins. This book will draw many persons closer to the great king, and his noble example, being made more realistic by the tie of relationship, cannot but be invigorating and purifying to them.

Lyon G. Tyler.

ILLUSTRATIONS.

Cover Design—The Golden Dragon, ... *W. C. West.*
Reade "Arms," . . . . *Jane C. Slaughter.*
Percy "Arms." . . . . " "
Mortimer "Arms. . . . . " "
Warner "Arms," . . . . " "
Howell "Arms," . . . . " "
Dymoke "Arms," . . . . *Bessie C. Grinnan.*
Lewis "Arms," . . . . " "
Robinson "Arms," . . . . " "
Westminster Hall.
Westminster Hall.
Tamworth Castle.
The King's Champion.
Marmion.
Charter of Tamworth Castle.
Alexander Robinson, ... *Old Portrait.*
Augustine Warner. . . . . *Old Portrait.*
Dymoke "Arms," with quarterings from "Scrivelsby."
Rose "Arms."
The Lion Gateway from "Scrivelsby."
Brass in Chapel from "Scrivelsby."
Neville "Arms."

AUTHORITIES.

Green's History of the English People.

Alfred the Great. By Sir Walter Besant and others.

Annals of the House of Percy. By Edward Barrington De Fonblanque.

Scrivelsby. By Reverend Samuel Lodge, M. A.

Americans of Royal Descent. Browning.

William and Mary College Quarterly.

Virginia Historical Magazine.

Weir's History of Horncastle.

W. Jones' Crowns and Coronations.

Banks' History of the Marmyuns.

Palmer's History of the House of Marmion.

London Encyclopædia.

Sharon Turner's History of the Anglo-Saxons.

National Dictionary of Biography.

Gentleman's Magazine, 1790, 1821, 1802.

Burke's History of the Commoners.

Burke's Peerage.

Curiosities of Popular Customs. Walsh.

Benjamin Rush. Court of St. James.

Burke's Landed Gentry.

Strickland's Queens of England

Hume's History of England.

Cabells and Their Kin. Alexander Brown.

Lancelot's Queens of England.

Hughes' Alfred the Great.

Le Neve's Pedigrees of Knights.

County Records. Land Grants.

Hotten's List of Emigrants.

History of the Ancient Ryedales. By Rev. G. T. Ridlon.

Proem.

The divine command, "Honor thy father and thy mother," may not be limited in its application to one generation. Its influence should lead to the honoring of our most remote ancestors—to the emulation of their virtues and the avoidance of their vices; to a recognition of the efforts made by them for the betterment of mankind, and a loyal pride in all the good by them accomplished.

Thou art no aimless drift from wreck of ocean,
  Upon a shore unconscious, idly cast.
Thou art inheritor of primal forces!
  To-day holds in solution all the Past!

ANNAH ROBINSON WATSON.

MEMPHIS, TENN.

A ROYAL LINEAGE:

ALFRED THE GREAT.

901–1901.

IT is claimed by many ancient writers that about the time of the Christian era a war-like prince of Asia left his kingdom near the Black Sea and came, with a mighty band of followers, to the Northwestern peninsula of Europe.

According to these early historians, he established rule over a vast extent of country, which was inherited by his posterity, and nine generations later his descendant Cerdic founded the Kingdom of Wessex, 519.

Of this kingdom, Winton Ceaster was the capital, and here was established the "Sanctuary of the house of Cerdic and Minster of the West Saxons." The present Cathedral of Winchester, begun in 1079, consecrated 1093, is supposed to stand upon the same spot as the edifice of Cerdic, and a still earlier temple built by the Romans.

Christianity in Britain was already several centuries old, for three British bishops were present at the Council of Arles, in Gaul, A. D. 314. The ruined Abbey of Glastonbury, in Somerset, is called "the cradle of British Christianity," but just at what date it was established may not be positively stated. About the time of Cerdic or his immediate descendants the place was known as Ynys Avallon, or the Isle of Avallon. Here was the home of King Arthur, and here gathered his knights of the "Table Round," here was Arthur laid to rest, and hither came King Henry the Second to visit his sacred tomb. Here assembled in 1897 bishops of the Anglican communion from all parts of the world, and in this year of our Lord, 1901, have some of the sacred stones from the ruins of Glastonbury been brought to America to be used as a memorial in the Cathedral of Washington. It is a solemn and significant thought that the Church of God bears testimony through these historic stones to an existence which dates back to a period only a few centuries later than the life of the Saviour; bears testimony to the continuity of the church and to the hereditary religious legacy of her children. Descending from Cerdic came Cynric, Ceawlin, Cuthwin, Cutha, Ceolwald, Cenred, Ingild, Eoppa, Eafa, Ealhmund, King of Wessex, and Egbert, 800-836.

Egbert, King of Wessex, married Raedburh. 800-836.

This Egbert, King of Wessex and grandfather of Alfred the Great, spent many years during his youth at the court of Charlemagne. Here he found the best opportunities for culture and training offered by the age in which he lived, and, making good use of them, developed into a wise and broad-minded ruler of his people.

Ethelwolf, son of Egbert and his wife, Raedburh, married Osburga, daughter of Oslac, cup-bearer to Egbert, King of Wessex. 836-858.

Ethelwolf, son of Egbert, King of Wessex, succeeded his father. He was of a pious and studious habit; made many journeys to Rome, and donated to the Roman See large sums from his royal income. After the death of his first wife, Osburga, he married Judith, daughter of Charles le Bald. The rare books of this monarch were among the wonders of the age. His illuminated Gospels bound in ivory were marvels of beauty, and some of the riches of his library are yet preserved in the collections of Paris.

Judith doubtless exercised a distinct and formative influence upon the character of her young stepson, for she carried with her to

Ethelwolf.

the court of Ethelwolf the impress of an environment unusual for its culture and learning.

Alfred "the Great," son of Ethelwolf and his wife, Osburga, married the Lady Ealhswyth, daughter of Ethelred Mucil, Earl of Gaini, in Mercia. 849-901.

Alfred the Great was born at the Palace of Wantage, and buried at Winton Ceaster, or Winchester. He died in 901, and the world has now, in 1901, reached the one thousandth anniversary of that event. Looking back over this period, it is fitting that all students, and more especially those who trace their lineage to this monarch, should pause to do him reverence; in the words of the English Laureate—

"Some lights there be within the heavenly spheres,
Yet unrevealed, the interspace so vast;
So through the distance of a thousand years,
Alfred's full radiance shines on us at last."

At an early age Alfred accompanied his father, Ethelwolf, to Rome. Here he resided during a period of some length, and was doubtless instructed in the languages, in poesy and music. It is said that later he traveled much in his own country, and so probably it chanced that he met the fair Lady

Alfred the Great.

Ealhswyth, daughter of an Earl of Mercia, and descended through her mother from the early Mercian kings. It is said that the wooing and wedding were somewhere in the Lincolnshire of to-day; that the devoted pair tarried in Ealhswyth's home for a time, and that when duty summoned the future king of Wessex elsewhere, the young wife remained in her father's halls until Alfred was ready to have her join him. This she did during his winter in lonely Athelnaye, "Isle of Princess," and in these darkest hours of his life she was doubtless his greatest solace. From this desolate habitation, surrounded by forest and morass, Alfred came forth when the winter had passed, with a scant following, and unfurled his banner, on which blazed the "Golden Dragon," "a hero as bold as Launcelot and as spotless as Galahad."

The Golden Dragon had long been the standard of his people, some authorities claiming that it was brought to Britain by the Romans; some that it was the standard of Arthur Pendragon, of the Table Round, the Welsh king, whose followers were vanquished by the warriors of Wessex.

Alfred the Great.

It seems to have been sometimes a great metal figure fastened to a staff, and borne before the conquering hosts, but upon the standard of Alfred is thought to have been embroidered in gold by the fair Ealhswyth.

The Golden Dragon is said to have led the Saxons in the battle of Hastings; the army of Henry the Seventh on the field of Bosworth, and also to have been used by Henry the Eighth and Queen Elizabeth.

The period of isolation upon the "Isle of Princess" had been as well a period of meditation and preparation, and Alfred now entered upon a time of intense physical and intellectual activity. His soul was fired by the high resolve which never, through all his after life, wavered, nor lost its dominant power—to serve his subjects to the utmost, to uplift. enlighten, ennoble and Christianize them. "King by the grace of God" was the thought ever in his mind, and armored in the grace of God did he go forth to do battle with the enemies of his people.

Probably his greatest gift was a rare administrative ability, a capacity to bring order out of chaos, to make a wise adjust-

Alfred the Great.

ment, and use of materials at hand. He occupied a lofty pinnacle of observation, from which he commanded the forces under him, and though the victim of a serious physical ailment, devoted himself unremittingly to the labors undertaken.

Through a many-sided character richly dowered with a variety of gifts, he reached out to all the interests and needs of his people. He was a wise master-builder of a nation, and withal a warrior, a law-giver, a Christian, and a man "who reverenced his conscience as his king." He was also a forceful writer; in truth, he was the father of English prose.

Had he done nothing for posterity beyond his contributions to literature, he would even then deserve to be called "great," for the literary movement, in a sense reformation, which he inaugurated, swept in ever-widening circles from his day to that of the Conquest.

He prefaced his code of laws with the words, "Thus saith the Lord, I am the Lord thy God." It was followed by the divine injunction, "Whatsoever ye would that men should do to you, do even so to them."

Alfred the Great.

He left many wise sayings, some of which are colored by the sadness so often found in the meditations of philosophers. "Desirest thou power," he said, "but thou shalt never obtain it without sorrows—sorrows from strange folk, and yet keener sorrows from thine own kindred." Again, "He who will investigate fame wisely and earnestly will perceive how little it is, how precarious, how frail, how bereft it is of all that is good."

Somewhat the same spirit is discovered in portions of his verse. The following is taken from the jubilee edition of his works:

> " Worldliness brought me here
>   Foolishly blind,
> Riches have wrought me here
>   Sadness of mind;
> When I rely on them,
>   Lo they depart—
> Bitterly, fie on them!
>   Rend they my heart."

He was "every inch a king," and gifted far above his fellows with graces of mind and body. Throughout all his years he wore "the white flower of a blameless life," and coming upon the hour in which was to be relinquished his earthly tabernacle, laid him

Alfred the Great.

down calmly, saying, "I have sought to live worthily the while I lived, and after my life to leave to the men that come after me a remembering of me in good works."

American institutions were builded, at least in some degree, by men who shared the blood of Alfred the Great; they will be upheld and protected by men who revere and hold sacred this noble heritage.

It is the record of such lives that "feeds the high tradition of the world," the emulation of such virtues as he made manifest that will nourish and stimulate to highest development the manhood of the race. Through one thousand years has throbbed his deathless influence—the realms of letters, of education, of science, of religion have widened and deepened, and reached upward in response to the impulse imparted by his transcendent personality.

If the race aspires to the possession of heroes in the future, it must honor its heroes of the past, and highest on the roll of heroes must be placed the name of the "hero king of Wessex, the hero founder of England."

Edward "the Elder," son of Alfred the Great and his wife, Ealhswyth, married Edgiva. 901–925.

During the continuous and successful action against the Danes which characterized the reign of Edward, he proved himself a wise as well as war-like prince. He was notably assisted by the intelligence and prudence of his noble sister, the Lady Ethelfleda, widow of Ethelbert, Earl of Mercia. Edward "the Elder" was the first of his line to claim the title "Rex Anglorum." His daughter, Princess Edgiva, married Charles the Third, King of France. From them descended, in the sixth generation, Elizabeth or Isobel de Vermandois.

Edmund "the First," son of Edward "the Elder" and his wife, Edgiva, married Elgiva. 940–946.

Edmund "the First" reigned less than six years, but during this period, among other notable deeds, he conquered Cumberland, and conferred it upon the King of Scotland. In exchange, the Scots were to protect England on the north from the Danes, and their king to do homage to Edmund. Edmund was assassinated in his own hall by Leofu, a notorious robber, whom he had banished.

Edgar, son of Edmund "the First" and his wife, Elgiva, married Aelfthryth. 958–975.

The reign of Edgar was undisturbed by domestic tumult or foreign invasion, which was probably due to the fact that he kept a large armament, both military and naval. This period is notable for the supremacy acquired by the Benedictine monks.

Ethelred "the Unready," son of Edgar and his wife, Aelfthryth, married Emma of Normandy. 979-1016.

Ethelred "the Unready" was one of the most cruel monarchs the English throne has known. He married in 1001 Emma, daughter of Richard (third Duke of Normandy, and grandson of Rollo the Ganger), and his second wife, Gunnor. After the death of Ethelred, Emma married Canute.

Edmond "Ironsides," son of Ethelred "the Unready" and his wife, Emma of Normandy, married Sigeferth. 1016.

Edmond was noted for his hardy valor, but during so short a reign had but scant time to prove his noble parts. He held the crown only from April to November, 1016, when he was murdered through the machinations of Edric, Duke of Mercia.

Edward, called "the Outlaw," son of Edmond "Ironsides" and his wife, Sigeferth, married Agatha, a German Princess. He died 1057.

Edward had lived many years in Hungary when recalled by his uncle, Edward "the Confessor." Only a few days after returning to England with his three children, the Atheling Edgar, Margaret, and Christina, he died. In Edgar the male Saxon line became extinct. Christina entered a convent.

Margaret Atheling, daughter of Edward and his wife, Agatha, married Malcolm Canmore, King of Scots. 1055–1093.

Malcolm Canmore was son of Duncan, king of Scots, who was murdered by Macbeth. His mother was the daughter of Siward, Earl of Northumberland, spoken of by Shakespeare as "Warlike Siward." He was descended from a long line of royal ancestors, extending back to Heremon, King of Ireland, 580 B. C., who is said to have married the Princess Tea-Tephi, a direct descendant of King David of Israel.

Margaret, called the "Saint," and her husband Malcolm, originated many notable enterprises in Scotland. They founded the famous Dunfermline Abbey, and there established Culdee monks, followers of St. Columba. Later these were succeeded by the canons regular of St. Augustine. It is

Margaret Atheling. claimed that with the Princess Tea-Tephi were brought to Ireland many priceless relics showing the Hebrew identity and royal descent of her people, among them the Jodham Morani, or priest's breast-plate, the harp of King David, Sweet Singer of Israel, and the famous coronation stone of the Kings of Ireland, Scotland and England. This stone, tradition states, is the identical pillow upon which the head of Jacob rested at Bethel; that it was carried to Egypt by his sons, and became sacred in the eyes of their descendants. It is called "The Stone of Fate," or fortune, and spoken of in old records as "the ancientest respected monument in the world." It was carried from Ireland to Scotland before the reign of Kenneth, A. D. 854. This Kenneth, ancestor of Malcolm Canmore, found it enclosed in a wooden chair at Dunstaffnage, a royal castle, and removed it to the Abbey of Scone. Here for four hundred and fifty years "all kingis of Scotland was crownit upon it, or quhil ye time of Robert Bruse. In quhais tyme, besides mony other crueltis done by kyng Edward, Lang Schankis, the said chair of Merbyll wes taik in be Inglismen and brocht

Margaret Atheling.

out of Scone to London, and put into Westmonister quhaer it remanis to our dayes." An ancient Irish prophecy declared, "The race of Scots of the true blood, if this prophecy be not false, unless they possess the Stone of Fate, shall fail to obtain regal power." King Kenneth had these words carven on the stone, and there they remain to this day—

"Or Fate is blind,
Or Scots shall find,
Where'er this stone
A royal throne."

Edward the First brought the magic stone to England, and built for it the chair, in which it may still be seen. Since the time of Edward, England's sovereigns have received their crowns seated here, a robe of cloth of gold being thrown over the wood which encases the stone. It was used at the coronation of Queen Victoria, and again in her jubilee festivities.

Matilda of Scotland, daughter of Margaret Atheling and her husband, Malcolm Canmore, King of Scots, married Henry First of England, who died 1135.

Henry the First was the son of William the Conqueror and his wife, Matilda, daughter of Baldwin, Count of Flanders, and his wife, Princess Adelaide, daughter of Robert, King of France. She was also a descendant of the mighty Charlemagne, who was not only one of the greatest rulers the world has known, but a Christian and an apostle of culture in the highest sense. His court was a centre of refinement and education, and its fame was disseminated to such distant parts that the great Caliph, Haroun-al-Rashid, sent in 801 an embassy to bear him gifts and greeting. His aims and aspirations were lofty, and the world has not yet ceased to pay homage to his genius.

William the Conqueror, Duke of Normandy, was sixth in descent from Rollo the Ganger and his wife, Giselle. This marriage took place soon after the appearance of Rollo in France, about the same time he received baptism, and became a Christian ruler of a Christian people.

That was a notable race which found its fullest expression and most complete type in the person of William the Conqueror. His ancestor, Rollo the Northman, with his

Matilda of Scotland.

followers set foot upon the shores of a foreign land, which soon received its name from him, and declared to the listening world, "We shall remain its masters and its lords!" And on the spot where he is supposed to have stood July 885, stands to-day a noble statue erected in his honor.

Matilda, daughter of Matilda of Scotland and her husband, King Henry First of England, married Geoffrey Plantagenet, Count of Anjou, who died 1151.

To Matilda was left by will all the possessions of her father, Henry the First, of England, but the throne was usurped by her cousin Stephen. Upon his death it reverted to Henry the Second, the son of Matilda and her husband, Geoffrey Plantagenet. Geoffrey was the most accomplished knight of his time. The surname, "Plantagenet," which he, as well as so many English sovereigns, bore, was derived from "planta genista," the Spanish broom plant. A sprig of this plant was worn in the cap of an ancestor of the house of Anjou on his pilgrimage to the Holy Land.

MR. DYMOKE, THE KING'S CHAMPION.

[From *An Authentic History of the Coronation of His Majesty King George the Fourth*, by Robert Huish, Esq., 1821.]

King Henry Second, son of Matilda and her husband, King Henry First of England, married Eleanor, Countess of Poitou and Aquitaine.
1133–1189.

Eleanor, Countess of Poitou and Aquitaine, was daughter of Count Guileme.

Besides being sovereign of her native dominions, she was, by hereditary right, chief reviewer and critic of the poets of Provence. At certain festivals held by her, called "Courts of Love," were recited all new "chansons" by the troubadours. She, with the ladies of her court, sat in judgment, and pronounced sentence regarding their literary merit. She was herself a popular lyric poet, and is counted among the authors of France.

King John, "Lackland," son of Henry Second and his wife, Eleanor of Poitou and Aquitaine, married Countess Isabella of Angouleme.
1167–1216.

Isabella of Angouleme was the daughter of Aymer de Taillifer, Count of Angouleme, and his wife, the Lady Alice de Courtenaye. Through her mother, who was a daughter of Peter de Courtenay, son of Louis the Sixth of France, she shared the blood of the Capetian line. The marriage of this princess with King John occurred in August, 1200, and was the precursor, for the royal pair, of a stormy life, both domestic and political. King John was cruel, selfish and indolent.

King John.

Isabella was beautiful and correspondingly vain. The barons of the realm, driven to desperation by the outrages perpetrated by the king, came together at Runnymede, June 19, 1215, and wrested from him Magna Charta, the declaration "by which has ever since been protected the personal liberty and the property of all free men."

King Henry Third, son of John "Lackland" and his wife Isabella of Angouleme, married Princess Eleanor of Provence. 1207–1272.

Eleanor of Provence was the daughter of Raymond, Count of Berenger, and his wife, the Lady Beatrix (daughter of Thomas, Count of Savoy). Eleanor of Provence was noted for her intellectual gifts, and was a writer of graceful verse. She was also celebrated for her beauty, but was extravagant and despotic, and by no means popular with her subjects. She survived her husband many years, and was very tenderly cared for by her son, Edward the First. Late in life she took the veil at the Monastery of Ambresbury.

King Edward First, son of Henry Third and his wife, Princess Eleanor of Provence, married Princess Eleanor of Castile. 1239–1307.

Princess Eleanor, surnamed "The Faithful," was the daughter of Ferdinand Third, surnamed the "Saint," King of Castile and Leon. Ferdinand was a wise and generously endowed monarch, and his children, Eleanor and Alphonso Tenth, inherited to a marked degree his intellectual qualities. Eleanor accompanied her royal husband, Edward First, on his pilgrimage to the Holy Land, and when her ladies would have dissuaded her, she replied, "Nothing should part those whom God hath joined. The way to heaven is as near, if not nearer, from Syria as from England or my native Spain."

King Edward Second, son of Edward First and his wife, Princess Eleanor of Castile, married Princess Isabella of France. 1284–1327.

Isabella of France was daughter of Philip le Bel, King of France, and his wife, Jane, Queen of Navarre. She was second cousin to the notorious King Charles the Bad, of Navarre, and much resembled him in character, being vain, selfish, cruel and insincere. The latter years of her life were spent in well-deserved imprisonment, and she died at Castle Rising, 1358. Edward the Second was weak and vacillating. He died early, and left no mark for good upon his age.

King Edward Third, son of Edward Second and his wife, Princess Isabella of France, married the Lady Philippa of Hainault. 1312–1377.

Philippa of Hainault was daughter of William, Count of Hainault and Holland, and his wife, Joanna, granddaughter of Philip the Third of France. She is described by Froissart as "the most courteous, liberal, and noble lady that ever reigned in her time." When dying she made several requests of her royal husband, who sat by her side clasping her hand and weeping. At the last she said, "I beg that when it shall please God to call you hence, you will choose no other sepulchre than mine, and that you will lie by my side in the Cloisters of Westminster Abbey."

Edward the Third was a most royal personage, and left notable works behind him. He conferred lasting benefits upon his people, was the father of English commerce, and the author of one of the most popular laws enacted by any prince of earlier or later days. This was the statute which defined the crime and limited the cases of high treason. Windsor Castle was built by his order. The sons of Edward the Third and his wife, Philippa of Hainault, were Edward, the Black Prince; William, who died in infancy; Lionel, Duke of Clarence; John of Gaunt, Duke of Lancaster; Edmund, Duke of York, and Thomas, Duke of Gloucester.

Lionel, Duke of Clarence, son of Edward Third and his wife, Philippa of Hainault, married the Lady Elizabeth de Burgh. He died 1368.

Elizabeth de Burgh was daughter of William de Burgh, Earl of Ulster, and his wife, the Lady Maud Plantagenet, granddaughter of Sir Patrick Chaworth. She was descended from Charlemagne, Henry the Third, and Cavbill Croodverg, the "red-hand King of Connaught." It would seem to be the latter to whom reference is made in the legend which relates that three vikings of early days went in their individual ships toward the island now known as Ireland. When approaching the shore, they agreed that he who first touched the land should own it; seeing himself outstripped in the race, one of the warlike contestants struck off his left hand and hurled it, red and bleeding, far ashore. Thus he first touched the land, and to him it belonged. Warlike clans descending from him used the "red-hand" on their shields and standards. The crest of the Lewis family of Virginia is a "red-hand," and since they are lineally descended from this King of Connaught, this legend possibly explains the crest.

Lionel, Duke of Clarence, was third son of Edward Third, and is said, of all the children of this monarch, most to have

Lionel, Duke of Clarence.

resembled him and the noble "Black Prince," who died in 1370. The second son, William, also died, and thus Lionel, Duke of Clarence, became the elder son; but John of Gaunt, "Time-honored Lancaster," secured the succession for his son, Henry the Fourth, thus defrauding Mortimer, the descendant of Lionel, Duke of Clarence. Generations later, Elizabeth of York, descendant of Lionel, Duke of Clarence, married Henry Seventh, descendant of John of Gaunt. So in Henry the Eighth the line of Edward the Third was doubly represented. Through this marriage Queen Victoria was descended from Lionel, Duke of Clarence, as well as from John of Gaunt.

Lady Philippa Plantagenet, daughter of Lionel, Duke of Clarence, and his wife, Elizabeth de Burgh, married Edmund Mortimer, Earl of March.

Edmund Mortimer was son of Roger de Mortimer, Earl of March, who died in 1360, and his wife, Lady Joan, daughter of Sir Peter Greenville, Lord of Trim Castle. He was descended from Llewelyn ap Lowerth, a great prince of North Wales, who married Lady Joan of England. Their daughter, the Princess Gladuse, married Ralph Mortimer, fifth Baron of Wigmore. Roger Mortimer,

ACQUIRIT QUI TUETUR.
MORTIMER.

Esperance en Dieu
PERCY

Lady Philippa Plantagenet.

son of Lady Philippa, and her husband, Edmund Mortimer, Earl of March, was heir-apparent, and named by his counsin Richard as his successor, but the throne was usurped by Henry Fourth.

Lady Elizabeth Mortimer, daughter of Lady Philippa Plantagenet and her husband, Edmund Mortimer, Earl of March, married Sir Henry Percy ("Hotspur"), who was killed in the battle of Shrewsbury. 1366–1403.

Sir Henry Percy, born May 20, 1366, was knighted when only twelve years of age. He was the son of Henry Percy, fourth Lord Alnwick, first Earl of Northumberland (born 1334; killed in battle of Branham Moor, 1408) and his first wife, Lady Margaret Neville, daughter of Lord Neville, of Raby Castle, and sister of the first Earl of Westmoreland. The Percies held large estates in Normandy, prior to the entrance of Rollo the Dane. It is said that the head of the house was baptized with Rollo at Rouen by the Bishop of Rheims, 912. They came to England the year after the conquest, and William Algernourne de Percy, the first of the name in England, is said to have founded Whitby Abbey. They were a warlike race, and ever in the forefront of the contests of

Lady Elizabeth Mortimer.

their time. While hot of temper, they were loyal and brave of heart, and left a record of which their posterity may well be proud. When Henry the Fourth sent an unjust demand to "Hotspur" for certain prisoners, Shakespeare thus voices his characteristic reply:

> "An' if the devil come and roar for them,
> I will not send them; I will after straight
> And tell him so; for I will ease my heart.
> Albeit I make a hazard of my head."

"Hotspur" was slain in the battle of Shrewsbury, and as evidence of the victory achieved by the undoing of so powerful a foe, Henry the Fourth ordered that he be decapitated on the field, and that his body be bound upright between two mill-stones, "so as all men might see that he was dead." His head was placed on the wall of Shrewsbury, and his quarters distributed among different northern cities, but subsequently the mutilated remains of the brave warrior were collected and delivered to his widow.

Henry Percy, Second Earl of Northumberland, son of Sir Henry Percy, "Hotspur," and his wife, Lady Elizabeth Mortimer, married Lady Eleanor Neville. 1394–1455.

Lady Eleanor Neville was daughter of Ralph Neville, first Lord of Westmoreland, and his wife, Joan de Beaufort, daughter of John of Gaunt and his wife, Catherine Swynford (the latter was widow of Sir Otis Swynford, and daughter of Sir Roger Roet of Hainault). Eleanor and her husband had twelve children. He was killed in the battle of St. Albans, 1455.

Henry Percy, Third Earl of Northumberland, son of Henry Percy, second Earl of Northumberland, and his wife, Lady Eleanor Neville, married Lady Eleanor Poynings. 1421–1461.

Lady Eleanor Poynings was daughter of Sir Richard Poynings, who fell at the siege of Orleans, 1429. She was the sole heiress of her grandfather, Lord Robert Poynings.

Lady Margaret Percy, daughter of Henry Percy, third Earl of Northumberland, and his wife, Lady Eleanor Poynings, married Sir William Gascoigne.

Sir William Gascoigne was son of Sir William Gascoigne and his wife, Lady Joan de Neville; she was daughter of John de Neville and his wife, Mary de Ferras, and granddaughter of Earl Robert de Ferras. She was also a descendant of John of Gaunt.

Lady Elizabeth Gascoigne, daughter of Lady Margaret Percy and her husband, Sir William Gascoigne, married Sir George Talbois, of Kyme, in Lincolnshire.

Sir George Talbois, Knight, is said to have descended from Ivo de Taillebois, a Norman follower of William the Conqueror, from whom he received large grants of land. He was also descended from Gilbert de Umfraville, Malcolm, Earl of Angus, the Earl of Buchan and Gilbert Barraden. He was the son of Sir Robert Talbois and grandson of Sir William Talbois, who married Elizabeth, daughter of Lord Bonville, 1438, and was knighted by Henry the Sixth in 1460 for distinguished services in the battle of St. Albans.

Sir George Talbois was also the father of Baron Gilbert Talbois, who died during the reign of Queen Elizabeth without issue, when the barony became extinct. His sister, Lady Anne Dymoke, was one of his heirs.

DYMOKE.

Lady Anne Talbois, daughter of Elizabeth Gascoigne and her husband, Sir George Talbois, married Sir Edward Dymoke, Hereditary Champion of England. He died 1566.

Lady Anne was fifth daughter of Sir George Talbois and his wife, Elizabeth Gascoigne. The arms borne by her house were quartered with those of Barraden, Fitzwith and Umfraville.

Sir Edward Dymoke was son and heir of Robert Dymoke of Scrivelsby Court, Lincolnshire, and his wife, Lady Anne Sparrow. He was a direct descendant of King Edward the First and his second wife, Princess Margaret, daughter of Philip le Hardi of France, through their son, Thomas Plantagenet of Brotherton, Earl of Norfolk, who wedded Lady Alice Halys; also through the Princess Joan de Acres, who wedded Gilbert, called the "Red Earl," of Clare. He was also related to the noble lines of de Mowbray, de Audley, Segrave and Stafford. His wife, Lady Anne Talbois, was descended from two sons of Edward the Third—Lionel, Duke of Clarence, and John, Duke of Lancaster.

Sir Edward Dymoke numbered amongst his ancestors Robert Marmyun, Lord of Castle Fontenaye in Normandy, and of Tamworth and Scrivelsby Court in England. Lord Robert Marmyun was descended from Rollo the Dane, and was Hereditary Cham-

Lady Anne Talbois. pion to his kinsman, William, Duke of Normandy, by whose side he fought upon the field of Hastings.

When the battle was over, William, now "The Conqueror," gathered his retainers about him upon the eminence, which had been marked by the most desperate fighting, and doubtless Robert de Marmyum, his Champion, held the nearest place to the royal person. It was on this night, with the dead and dying piled in great heaps about the Standard, that William declared his intention of building upon the bloody field a great Battle Abbey. Lord Marmyum appeared as Champion of England at the double coronation of William and Matilda, April, 1068, at Winchester. The challenge upon this occasion was delivered in the following words: "If any person deny that our most gracious sovereigns, Lord William and his spouse Matilda, are King and Queen of England he is a false-hearted traitor and a liar, and here I, as Champion, do challenge him to single combat."

Thus it appears that the august office of Royal or Hereditary Champion to the King was in England a continuation of the office

TAMWORTH

Hic per Willielmum Conquestorem Robertus Marmion Dominus Castelli Efficitur.

Lady Anne Talbois.

as already existing in the Dukedom of Normandy.

When King William rewarded his Norman followers, a number of estates were given to this Robert de Marmyum. Among them was Tamworth, a parliamentary and municipal borough, partly in Stafford, partly in Warwickshire. Of this estate Sir William Dugdale wrote:

"This Castle, being in the hands of King William, after his Conquest, was by him given unto Robert Marmion, as is verified by an ancient window of this church, where the same King, being depicted in his Robes of State and Crowned, stretcheth forth his hand to him, holding a Charter therein, near the Gate of a Faire Castle, an exact representation whereof I have in Page 822 exhibited."

Scrivelsby Court, a baronial fief, was conferred upon Robert Marmyon according to the then existing legal forms, with a special condition annexed to the tenure, that it should be held by the particular service of himself, and the heirs of the fee, performing the office of Champion to every sovereign of England. The Dymokes inherited Scrivelsby Court, or Manor, from this Sir Robert

Lady Anne Talbois.

Marmyun, and it has been owned by them through all the succeeding centuries. It is situated in the most picturesque portion of Mid-Lincolnshire, and is one of the most unique establishments in England.

The buildings are frónted by a park, the entrance to which is marked by a high arch of grey stone, overgrown with ivy. Standing upon the arch, in bold relief, is the figure of a lion, life-size. The lion is one of the crests of the Dymokes, and their "arms" show two "lions passant" upon a black field, with the motto "Pro Rege Dimico." The lion was used from early times as the royal symbol of England, Normandy and Scotland, and doubtless became the property of the Dymokes as Champions of the Crown.

Scrivelsby Chapel is a small quaint building, some portions of which are at least five hundred years old. Some one describing it a number of years ago, said, "Among the tombs is that of Sir Robert Dymoke, Champion of Richard Third, Henry Seventh and Eighth. On the top of the tomb is a plate of brass on which his figure is sculptured in full armour in recumbent posture, with his helmet under his head, and a lion at his feet.

Lady Anne Talbois.

Above the figure is a shield containing the family arms, and beneath, the following inscription: 'Here liethe the Body of Sir Robert Dymoke of Scrivelsby, Knight and Baronet, who departed out of this present lyfe the XX day of Apryle in ye yere of our Lord God MDLXV upon whose sowle Almighte god have m ci. Amen.' "

By prescriptive right the perquisites of the Champion were "one of the King's best coursiers, the second best in the royal stables, with saddle, harness and trappings of cloth of gold: one of the King's best suits of armour, with cases of cloth of gold; and all other things belonging to the King's body when he goes into mortal combat." The golden cup and its cover, from which the King and the Champion drank each other's health, many yards of crimson satin, and other smaller articles were also his. The "arms" provided for Sir Charles Dymoke, royal Champion at the coronation of James the Second, 1685, are carefully enumerated by historians. They were "a complete suit of white armour, a pair of gauntlets, a sword and a hanger, a case of rich pistols, an oval shield with the Champion's arms painted on

Lady Anne Talbois.

it, and a gilded lance fringed about the handles, also a field saddle of crimson velvet with breast-plate and other caparisons for the horse, richly laden with gold and silver, a plume of red, white and blue feathers consisting of eighteen falls and a heron's top. Another plume for the horse's head and trumpet banners, with the Champion's own arms depicted on them."

The last official appearance of the Champion was at the coronation of George the Fourth; for the grand banquet, with this picturesque feature, was dispensed with at the coronation of King William, and also at that of Queen Victoria, though several later Dymokes have borne the title of "The Honorable the Queen's Champion." Francis Scaman Dymoke, the present owner of Scrivelsby, the ancestral estate, is nineteenth in the line of Royal Champions. His youthful son, Frank Dymoke, was born in the same year as Prince Edward of York, grandson of the present King, Edward the Seventh.

Dating, as this office does, from a period prior to the Conquest, and descending, through all succeeding centuries, hereditary

CORONATION OF GEORGE IV, IN WESTMINSTER HALL.

THE CHAMPION'S CHALLENGE.

From a Contemporary Engraving in the *Gentleman's Magazine*.

SOUTH VIEW OF WESTMINSTER HALL,

Representing the manner of serving up the first course at the Coronation Banquet.

Lady Anne Talbois. in one family, it appeals to the present age as the latest, most perfect, and most picturesque survival of the age of romance and chivalry. The influence of chivalry was to deeds of heroism and high emprise; it marked the transition period from the feudalism of violence to the feudalism of culture. It made the Crusades possible, and brought into existence a literature which claims the chronicles of Froissart and the songs and stories of medieval bards. It created legends through which the universal heart of the world found expression, and in which self-sacrifice as a potent factor in life stood arrayed against sordid and selfish considerations.

In the office of King's Champion was focused, to a certain extent, the multiform influences of chivalry, and through its picturesque ceremonies was exercised a force which faintly reaches even this utilitarian age of "sophisters, economists and calculators." This influence or force may be traced in some of the most delightful literature of England. In *Ivanhoe* there are many allusions which suggest that the knightly service of the Champion and the ancient "wager of battel," for which he stood, had aided in

Lady Anne Talbois.

formulating and directing the author's thought. In *Redgauntlet* the champion appears in person. In *Marmion,* Lord Robert Marmyun, it would seem, was, to some extent at least, the original of the picture drawn, and his home, Tamworth Castle, is frequently mentioned.

> "Marmion, whose steady heart and eye
> Ne'er changed in worst extremity,
> Marmion, whose soul could scantly brook
> E'en from his King a haughty look;
> Whose accent of command controlled
> In camps, the boldest of the bold."

There can be no reasonable doubt that Scrivelsby, with its unique traditions, exerted a powerful influence over the imagination of Lord Tennyson. There was here for the super-sensitive consciousness of the poet an intangible, pervasive, intoxicating, psychic influence through which the scenes of the past were invoked, and through which the principles which had given it existence were conjured up as a force in his own life. Somersby, the childhood home of the Laureate, was only seven miles from Scrivelsby Manor. It is said that the stately park of the latter, its wide-stretching wolds and meadows, were

TAMWORTH CASTLE.

Taken from the foot of "Lady Bridge," and drawn on the spot by Mr. Williams, an eminent portrait painter, in the year [illegible].

[*Gentleman's Magazine and Historical Chron…*

THE LION GATEWAY, SCRIVELSBY PARK.

Lady Anne Talbois. frequently the chosen scenes of his rambles, and in the Manor House were the rare old relics of armour and of knightly service upon which he so delighted to dwell. Here lived the descendants of King Alfred and the doughty Norman warriors, and many times must he have passed through the great Lion Gateway, which guarded the entrance to the park, and gazed upon the royal beast which stood erect upon its arch of solid masonry. The Dymokes of Scrivelsby were descended from Robert de Vere, Earl of Oxford, and in *Lady Clara Vere de Vere* the poet says:

"Nor would I break for your sweet sake,
A heart that dotes on truer charms,
A simple maiden in her flower
Is worth a hundred coats-of-arms.

. . . . .

"You sought to prove how I could love,
And my disdain is your reply.
The lion on your old stone gates
Is not more cold to you than I.

. . . . .

"Howe'er it be, it seems to me,
'Tis only noble to be good,
Kind hearts are more than coronets,
And simple faith than Norman blood."

The references here to the many coats-of-arms shown at Scrivelsby, the lion on "the

Lady Anne Talbois.

old stone gates," the long descent and Norman blood, are surely most suggestive.

In the chapel of Scrivelsby there is a memorial figure, a knight cross-legged; in *Locksley Hall Sixty Years After* are the lines:

"Yonder in that chapel, slowly sinking now into the ground,
Lies the warrior, my forefather, with his feet upon the hound.

"Crossed, for once he sailed the sea to crush the Moslem in his pride;
Dead the warrior, dead his glory, dead the cause in which he died.

. . . . .

"Here is Locksley Hall, my grandson, here the Lion-guarded gate.

. . . . .

"There is one old Hostel left us where they swing the Locksley shield,
Till the peasant cow shall butt the 'Lion passant' from his field."

The Dymoke shield bears "two lions passant." In the park at Scrivelsby is a leaden life-size figure of a cow, which has been there many years; doubtless it suggested the lines above.

BRASS TO LIONEL DYMOKE IN HORNCASTLE CHURCH

Lady Anne Talbois.

In connection with the interesting literature bearing upon this subject should be mentioned autograph letters from sovereigns of England to the various Champions. Among these is one from Henry the Eighth to Sir Robert Dymoke, dated 1513, and one from Queen Mary to Sir Edward.

There are also many curious old ballads, such as the one subjoined—

"The Norman Barons Marmyon
At Norman Court held high degree;
Brave Knights and Champions, every one,
To him who wone brave Scrivelsby.

"The Lincoln lands the Conqueror gave,
That England's glove they should convey,
To knight renowned among the brave,
The Baron bold of Fontenaye.

"The royal grant from sire to son,
Devolved direct in capite,
Until deceased Phil. Marmyon,
When rose fair Joan of Scrivelsby.

"And ever since when England's kings
Are diademed—no matter where—
The Champion Dymoke boldly flings
His glove, should treason venture there.

. . . . .

"Then bravely cry with Dymoke bold,
Long may the king triumphant reign,
And when fair hands the sceptre hold,
More bravely still—long live the Queen."

Lady Anne Talbois.

Among the most illustrious Champions were Philip Marmion, who served in the third Crusade, Sir Thomas Dymoke, who was beheaded, and Sir Robert Dymoke, who died in defence of his religion. This Sir Robert was one of the ten children of Sir Edward Dymoke, Champion for Edward the Sixth and Queens Mary and Elizabeth. He succeeded to the estates and titles, married the daughter of Edward Clinton, Earl of Lincoln, and was a conspicuous figure in the social life of his day. He was a brother of the Frances Dymoke (who married Thomas Windebank) whose descendant, George Reade, settled in Virginia.

The Dymokes had been staunch adherents of the Church of Rome, and during the religious disturbances which characterized the reign of Queen Elizabeth, Sir Robert stood firm and unflinching in defense of the faith in which he was born.

Queen Elizabeth, following the policy which led her to maintain in one county a bishop who adhered to Rome, in another one of pronounced Puritanical tendencies, had appointed for Lincoln one of the latter, and Sir Robert was ordered to appear before him

illiam and Philip Marmion were among the Barons who served in the third Crusade; they were feudal Lords of the barony of Tamworth, and of the manor of Scrivelsby in Lincolnshire: the latter was held by Grand Sergeantry to perform the office of Champion at the King's coronation. An effigy (cross-legged) of one of the above crusaders lies in the church at Scrivelsby. The male descendants of the Marmions are Sir Henry Dymoke, the Rev. John Dymoke, and his son Henry. The present Baronet is the seventeenth of the family who has inherited the manor of Scrivelsby with the office of Champion. Philip Marmion has a different bearing assigned to him in the transcript of the Roll of the Crusaders, by Ralph Brooke, 1563, No. 1,120 Ashmole Library, Oxford, where the arms are tricked argent; a sword, in pale sable.

Lady Anne Talbois. and answer charges that he maintained a Romish priest at Scrivelsby, and had mass celebrated in the chapel. Sir Robert was too ill to obey the summons, so the prelate came to him. Threats, promises, persuasions were of no avail. The old knight was not called to serve as Champion for an earthly sovereign, but he filled that office nobly in discharging his duty to a heavenly; and though ill and helpless, would not retract nor recant. As a result, he was forcibly taken from his bed and his manor house, carried to Lincoln prison and incarcerated. Here, from exposure and privation, he died the death of a hero, a champion for his faith to the last, wherefore he is called the "Martyr Champion."

> "The greatest gift the hero leaves his race
> Is to have been a hero."

To Sir Edward Dymoke and his wife, the Lady Anne Talbois, were born eleven children: Robert, Charles, Edward; Elizabeth, married to Henry Ayscough; Margaret, to Lord Eure; Frances, to Sir Thomas Windebank; Susan, to Sir Thomas Lambert; Dorothy, Sarah, Bridget and Arthur.

Lady Anne Talbois.

The last four names are not found in all the records, but Arthur is supposed to have been the father of Edward, who migrated to America, and was the father of Thomas Dymoke, who died at Barnstaple, Massachusetts, 1658. This Thomas Dymoke married Ann Hammond. They had several children, whose descendants are now living in different parts of America.

Frances, daughter of Sir Edward Dymoke and his wife, Lady Anne Talbois, married Sir Thomas Windebank, August 20, 1566.

Sir Thomas Windebank, who died 1607, was son of Sir Richard Windebank of Haines Hall, Berkshire, and his wife, Margaret (daughter of Griffith ap Henry). He was clerk of the signet to Queen Elizabeth and her successor, King James.

Mildred Windebank, daughter of Frances Dymoke and her husband, Sir Thomas Windebank, married Robert Reade.

Robert Reade was son of Andrew Reade, who died 1623, and his wife, ——— Cooke, of Kent. Their home was the Manor of Linkenholt, Hampshire, England.

George Reade, son of Mildred Windebank and her husband, Robert Reade, married Elizabeth Martian. 1600–1671.

Elizabeth Martian was daughter of Captain Nicholas Martian, of York County, Virginia, whose home occupied the present site of Yorktown. He was of French birth, but a naturalized citizen of England, from whence he came to Virginia about 1621, with a wife and two children. He married a second time, some time after 1625, Jane, widow of Lieutenant Berkely, and a third time, about 1645, Isabella Beech. He was Justice of York, Burgess for York and Kiskyache, and held other offices (see *Some Notable Families of America,* by Annah Robinson Watson). His will, dated March 1, 1656, recorded in York County April 24, 1657, divided his estate between his daughters, Elizabeth, wife of Colonel George Reade; Mary, wife of Lieutenant-Colonel John Scasbrook, and Sarah, wife of Captain William Fuller, Governor of Maryland.

Colonel George Reade came to America in 1637. He was Secretary to the Colony of Virginia in 1640, Burgess, member of His Majesty's Council, Colonel of Militia, (whence his title), and held other important offices. (For information, see *Some Notable Families of America.*)

Col. George Reade.

To Colonel George Reade and his wife, Elizabeth Martian, were born twelve children:

1. Mildred Reade, who married Colonel Augustine Warner.

2. George Reade, died without issue.

3. Robert Reade, married Mary Lilly, daughter of John Lilly, and granddaughter of John Lilly and his wife, Dorothy Wade (daughter of Armiger Wade and his wife, the heiress of Edward Malson, or Moulson, of York County). Margaret Reade, daughter of Robert Reade and his wife, Mary Lilly, married Thomas Nelson. They were grandparents of General Thomas Nelson. Samuel Reade, son of Robert and his wife, Mary Lilly, had a daughter, Frances, who married Anthony Robinson, High Sheriff for York County.

4. Francis Reade, married, first, Jane Chisman, and had Mary Reade (who married Edward Davis, of King and Queen County), and Elizabeth Reade, who married Paul Watlington. Francis Reade married, second, Anne ———, and had George, Anne and Benjamin.

5. Benjamin Reade, married Lucy ——.

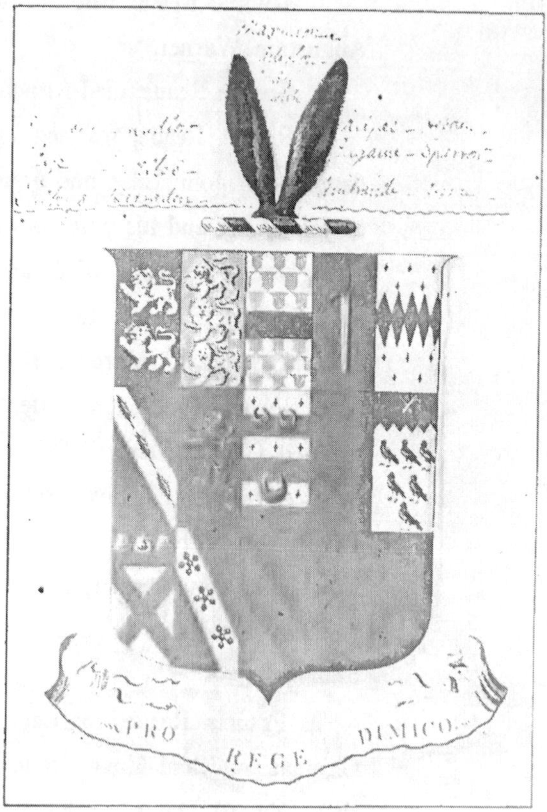

DYMOKE.

Col. George Reade. and had Gwynn Reade, who married Dorothy ——.

6. Thomas Reade, married Lucy Gwynn, daughter of Edmund Gwynn, of Gloucester County. They had eleven children: (1) Thomas, who died without issue. (2) Rev. John Reade, whose only daughter, Sarah, married John Rootes. (3) Lucy, who married John Dixon, of Bristol. (4) Mildred, who married Major Philip Rootes. (5) Mary, who married Mordecai Throckmorton. (6) Believed to be Colonel Clement Read, of Charlotte. Among the descendants of Colonel George Reade it is probable that none other was more largely dowered with the characteristics which for a thousand years had given his race preëminence than

Col. Clement Read,

who was born January 1, 1707. He was educated at William and Mary College: later was qualified as attorney in Goochland, Albemarle, and Brunswick Counties; was a vestryman in the churches of Brunswick and Lunenburg, trustee of William and

Col. George Reade. Mary College, 1729; first clerk of Lunenburg, 1746; was president of the Council, and upon the departure of Governor Gooch for England, 1749, acted as governor of the colony.

In 1730, he married Mary Hill, only daughter of William Hill, believed to have been an officer of the British navy, and descendant of the Marquis of Downshire and his wife, Priscilla, daughter of Edmund Jenings, Governor of Virginia.

The home of Colonel Clement Read and his wife, Mary Hill, was "Bushy Forest," near Charlotte Court-house, now Smithville. It was doubtless counted among the notable homesteads in those days, and a centre for both social and political activities, for Colonel Clement Read was one of the most influential men of his section, and his wife, a stately dame, who, like himself, was of noble lineage. Hundreds of slaves waited to do their bidding on this and other handsome estates, and the coach and four in which the mistress of the mansion took her pleasure drives or made her journeys was an object to be gazed upon with envy by less fortunate folk. The children of this marriage were:

Col. George Reade.

1. Colonel Clement Read, Jr., who married Mary Nash.

2. Colonel Isaac Read, who married Sarah Embry.

3. Colonel Thomas Read, who married Elizabeth Nash.

4. Major Edmund Read, who married, first, Miss Lewis; second, Paulina Cabell, daughter of Colonel William Cabell.

5. Capt Jonathan Read, who married Jane Lewis.

6. Mary Read, who married Thomas Nash. Their daughter, Ann Owen Nash, married Rev. John Cameron, of Petersburg, Virginia.

7. Margaret Read, who married Judge Paul Carrington; their eldest daughter, Mary, married Colonel S. W. Venable. Another daughter, Anne, married Colonel William Cabell, Jr.

8. Anne Read, who married, first, William Jameson; second, Richard Elliott.

Colonel Clement Read, Jr., was born 1736, and educated at William and Mary College; he read law under his father, and was appointed first clerk of Charlotte County. He married, in 1757, Mary Nash, daughter

Col. George Reade.

of Judge John Nash, of Templeton Manor (who was appointed colonel and chairman of the Committee of Safety from Prince Edward County). Their children were Clement, who served as lieutenant in the Revolution; John Nash, Thomas, Harrison and Mary.

The second son of this marriage, Captain John Nash Read, joined the Continental Army, under General Greene, at the age of eighteen, and served at Guilford Courthouse, Cowpens, and in other notable engagements.

He was married three times: first to Elizabeth Julia Spencer, a first cousin of Thomas Jefferson. Their children were Dr. Clement, Dr. John Harris, Major Sion Spencer, Martin, Dr. Thomas Hill, and seven daughters.

The second wife was Elizabeth Fisher Nash. The children of this union were James Allen and Francis Nash.

The third wife was Mary Barksdale. The children of this union were William Harrison, Nathaniel Barksdale, Edmund Randolph, Peter, and six daughters.

Captain John Nash Read moved, in 1806,

Col. George Reade.

from Charlotte County, Virginia, to Rutherford County, Tennessee; here he died in January, 1826.

Major Sion Spencer Read, a son of the first marriage of Captain John Nash Read, served in the war of 1812—first with Coffee's Regiment of Cavalry, and afterwards with Williamson's Regiment of mounted gunmen.

In 1819 he married Hardenia Jefferson Spencer, of Charlotte County, Virginia. Their children were Lycurgus, Dr. John Thomas, George Granville, Edwin Cole, Dr. Corin, Charles William, and two daughters.

In October, 1839, Major Sion Spencer Read moved to McMinnville, Tennessee.

Dr. John Thomas Read, son of Sion Spencer Read and his wife, Hardenia Jefferson Spencer, graduated from Jefferson Medical College, Philadelphia, in March, 1853. Prior to his studies here he had served in the Mexican war, and in the civil war he served with the Sixteenth Tennessee Regiment as surgeon, having the rank of major.

He married Laurena Caroline Rankin, daughter of David Rankin, of Sequatchie Valley, Tennessee. Their children were (1) Laura B., who married Samuel McCall, and

Col. George Reade.

had three sons. One of these, Wright McCall, is now living; the other two died in infancy. (2) Mary H., who married William W. Frater, and had four daughters. (3) Harriet S., who married Rev. H. H. Sneed, and had eight children. (4) Carrie R., who married Letcher Pickens, and had two sons, Henry Berlin and John Read. (5) Samuel Roberson Read, of Chattanooga, Tennessee, who married Lizzie Hamilton, daughter of Dr. P. D. Sims, also of Chattanooga. They had four children—Mary Hill, Elizabeth Nash, Margaret and Martin Sims.

Thomas Reade and his wife, Lucy Gwynne, had five other children, whose names are not known. Lucy Gwynne was granddaughter of Colonel William Bernard, a great-great-great-grandson of Lady Margaret le Scrope, who was great-great-great-great-great-granddaughter of Princess Joan de Acres and her husband, Gilbert de Clare. Among the great-grandchildren of Thomas Reade and Lucy Gwynne was Frances Throckmorton, who married General William Madison. They were great-great-grandparents of Susie Ashton Chapman Perkins.

Col. George Reade.

7. Elizabeth Reade, seventh child of Colonel George Reade and Elizabeth Martian, married Captain Thomas Chisman, of York County, Virginia. Their son, John Chisman, married Eleanor Howard. A daughter of this marriage, Diana, married James Goodwin.

The names of the other five children of Colonel George Reade, and his wife, Elizabeth Martian, are not known.

Mildred Reade, daughter of Col. George Reade and his wife, Elizabeth Martian, married Col. Augustine Warner, of "Warner Hall," Gloucester County, Virginia. He was born October 20, 1643; died June 10, 1681.

Colonel Augustine Warner was son of Captain Augustine Warner (who came to America prior to 1630) and his wife, Mary ——. He was educated at the "Merchant Tailors" School, London, and was later Burgess, Speaker of the House of Burgesses, Member of the Council, and Colonel of Militia. (For dates, see *Some Notable Families of America.*)

To Colonel Augustine Warner and his wife, Mildred Reade, were born Mildred, who married Laurence Washington (they were grandparents of George Washington). (2) Robert, who died without issue. (3)

Mildred Reade.

George, who died without issue. (4) Mary, who married John Smith, of Purton, and had Augustine Smith, who married Sarah Carver. Their daughter, Sarah Smith, married Robert Throckmorton, and had a son, Warner Throckmorton, who married Julia Langborne. Their daughter, Mary Throckmorton, married Dr. William Taliaferro; they were grandparents of William B. Taliaferro. (5) Elizabeth, who married Colonel John Lewis.

Elizabeth Warner, daughter of Mildred Reade and her husband, Col. Augustine Warner, married Col. John Lewis. She was born November 24, 1672; died 1719 or 1720.

Colonel John Lewis was the son of Major John Lewis and his wife, Isabella ——. (Major John Lewis owned estates in New Kent and Gloucester Counties, and in 1680 was Captain of Horse in the Militia of the former; he was also one of its justices. In 1685 he was a major in the foot service.)

Colonel John Lewis was born November 30, 1669; died November 14, 1725. He was a Member of the Council, 1715.

To him and his wife, Elizabeth Warner, were born fourteen children; the names of only eight of these have been preserved:

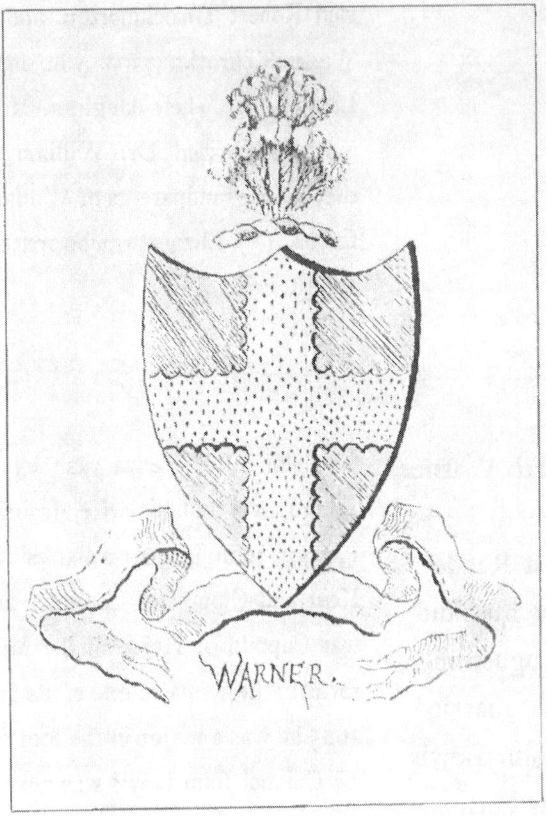
WARNER.

Elizabeth Warner.

Catharine, born ——; baptized November, 1702.

Elizabeth, born ——; baptized November, 1702.

John, born ——; baptized November, 1702; married Frances Fielding, daughter of Henry Fielding, of King and Queen County.

Charles (called Colonel Charles of "The Byrd"), born October 13, 1690; died 1779; married, 1717, Mary, daughter of John Howell, gentleman.

Robert (called Colonel Robert of "Belvoir"), born ——; baptized May 4, 1702; married Jane, daughter of Nicholas Meriwether and his wife, Elizabeth Crafford.

Elizabeth, born ——; baptized March 7, 1706.

Isabella, born ——; baptized December 18, 1707; married Dr. Thomas Clayton, July 14, 1720; had one child, who died young.

Anne, born ——; baptized February 14, 1712.

Colonel Charles Lewis,

Of "The Byrd."

Colonel Charles Lewis, son of Colonel John Lewis and his wife, Elizabeth Warner, was born October, 1696, and died in 1779. He married, in 1717, Mary Howell, daughter of John Howell, gentleman.

The home of Colonel Charles Lewis was the "Byrd Plantation," in Goochland County, which took its name from the limpid stream, "The Byrd," which flowed through its productive acres; but besides this, he had other and very valuable estates with many slaves and large herds of cattle. He was an officer in the French and Indian wars, a member of the Council, and a man of position and influence in his community. The children of Charles Lewis and his wife, Mary Howell, were:

HOWEL

1. John, who married Jane Meriwether, daughter of Colonel Robert Lewis and his wife, Jane Meriwether.

2. Charles, who married Mary, daughter of Isham Randolph.

3. Elizabeth, who married William Kennon, of Chesterfield County.

4. James, who married Isabella, or Elizabeth, surname thought to have been Taylor.

5. Howell, born September 13, 1731, died about 1814, married Isabella Willis, daughter of Colonel Henry Willis, the founder of Fredericksburg.

6. Ann, who married Edmund Taylor.

7. Robert, who married Jane Woodson, daughter of Tucker Woodson.

8. Frances, who married Robert Lewis, of Louisa County, son of Colonel Robert Lewis, of "Belvoir," and his wife, Jane Meriwether.

"The Byrd Plantation" became one of the notable colonial estates, and the life led by its family-circle was generous, hospitable, and far-reaching in its social influence. The children and grandchildren were allied by marriage to the leading families of the State, and wielded a strong power in both political and social circles. The will of Colonel Charles Lewis was probated in 1779, and is a most interesting document on account of the side-lights which it throws upon the life of that day, as well as upon his family relations.

He bequeaths to his "beloved wife, Mary Lewis," his whole estate, both real and personal, for her natural life. She is also named as executrix without bond. The will alludes to several different estates, to slaves and cattle, and mentions eight children by name. Many interesting heir-looms have come down to his descendants, the rarest of china and glass, and the quaintest of silver, all of which was doubtless brought in those early days from the mother country.

Howell Lewis, son of Colonel Charles Lewis, of "The Byrd," and his wife, Mary Howell, married Isabella Willis. They moved to Granville County, North Carolina, and established the home "Elmwood," which became a centre for one of the most cultured and patrician circles of the State. He served as major in the Revolution, and later was a member of the State Senate. His will was proved at the February court of Granville

AUGUSTINE WARNER.[2]

County, 1814. His wife survived him, and died in her eightieth year. Their children were:

1. Charles.

2. Willis.

3. Isabella, married ——— Jeffries.

4. Anne, married ——— Morton.

5. Frances, married ——— Bugg.

6. Jane, married David Hinton, of "The Oaks," Wake County, North Carolina, where still resides their great-granddaughter, Mary Hilliard Hinton.

7. Mildred, married John Cobb, first of Goochland County, Virginia, and then of Georgia. Their children were Howell Cobb (who was Secretary of the Treasury under Buchanan), Mary Willis Cobb, Susannah Cobb, John Addison Cobb and Mildred Cobb.

8. Mary, married ——— Kennon.

9. Elizabeth, married William Ridley, of Granville County, North Carolina.

10. Howell, born April 2, 1759; married, in 1780, Betsy Coleman, of Goochland County, Virginia, daughter of Robert Coleman.

Elizabeth Lewis married William Ridley. Their daughter, Mary Ridley, married Colonel Nathaniel Robards, of Granville County, North Carolina. He was descended from John Robards, who came from Wales in 1710, and settled in Goochland County, Va. His son, William, served on the Committee of Safety in 1776, and had at least six sons and two sons-in-law in the Colonial Army; one of the six sons, James, married Mary, daughter of Major Nathaniel Massie, and was father of Colonel Nathaniel Robards, who married Mary Ridley.

The Robards came of a race richly endowed with both mental and physical gifts. They were tall, graceful in bearing, courtly in demeanor, and while largely engaged in planting, were also devoted to intellectual pursuits. Colonel Nathaniel Robards lost by fire a rare collection of books and curios, among which were family records of great value inscribed upon vellum. To him and his wife, Mary Ridley, were born eleven children—

1. William H. Robards, born October 1, 1806; died March 6, 1862. He was a man whose many gifts, hereditary and acquired,

won a broad recognition, and at his home, "Bendemeer." assembled many who were distinguished in the highest circles. He served in the Confederate army as brigadier-general. His wife was Anne Eliza Toole, a woman of wealth, and conspicuous for her great beauty and social graces. Their daughter, Mrs. Lucius H. Terry, née Mary E. Robards, resides at New Orleans, Louisiana. She is a member of the Colonial Dames of America.

2. Eliza Robards, married Colonel James Wilkes; left three children. One of these is Dr. James Howell Wilkes, of Columbia, Tennessee.

3. Mary Ann Robards, married David Kerns; left three children. One of these is C. W. Kerns, of Gilmer, Texas.

4. Howell Ridley Robards was a man of unusual mental ability, a physician of highest reputation, and assistant surgeon in the Mexican war. He married Margaret E. Camp; left three children; one of these is W. C. Robards, of San Antonio, Texas.

5. Willis Lewis Robards (colonel in the Confederate Army), married Miss ——— Rude; left three children.

6. James Ridley Robards, assistant surgeon in Mexican war; died of wounds received in battle.

7. Caroline Virginia Robards, died young.

8. Francis Hawkes Robards, went to California during the gold fever; supposed to have died young.

9. Charles Lewis Robards, born April 11, 1827; died November 22, 1870. He served in the civil war as aide-de-camp on the staff of General Henry E. McCulloch, and married Julia Tabitha White, of Shreveport, Louisiana, who is descended from the families of Donelson, Owen, and Lowe, of Virginia, and Purnell, of Maryland. This Lowe family is said to be descended from John Lowe, the renowned Bishop of Rochester. Julia White is also descended from Abraham Sublette and his wife, Susannah Dupuy, French Huguenots. Susannah was sister to Bartholomew Dupuy, of the Body Guard of Louis XIV., who came to America in 1700. Charles Lewis Robards and his wife, Julia T. White, had one child, Mattie Robards, who married August Mayer, civil engineer and planter, now living in Shreveport,

Louisiana. Mrs. Mayer is a member of the Colonial Dames of America.

10. Julia Constance Robards, died young.

11. John Ridley Robards, died young.

Among the families mentioned in this sketch none is more worthy of attention than that of Ridley. The name, variously spelled, is found in the earliest records, and always as belonging to those of high estate and position.

An English authority claims that in Scandinavia it was derived in primitive times from a place called "Rugdal," that is, "Rye-dale," the Valley of Rye. From Scandinavia it would seem that some bearing the name went to France, for here Walgrinus Ridel was Earl of Angouleme and Piragord probably as early as 885. He was kinsman to Charles le Bald, King of France, and married Rosalind, daughter of the Duke of Aquitaine. Their descendant in the eighth generation is said to have been Galfridus Ridel, who followed William the Conqueror to

England. His oldest son, Galfridus Ridel, second, became Lord Justiciary of all England during the reign of Henry the First. He married Geva, daughter of the Earl of Chester, the nephew of William the Conqueror. From the time of the Norman Conquest the family held landed estates in England, and the name may be found on the Battle Abbey Roll and Dooms-day Book. Ridley Hall, Cheshire, as belonging to Bryon Ridley, was known in 1157.

It is claimed that the most ancient charter in existence issued by a king to a layman bears date 1125, and was bestowed by King David of Scotland upon a member of this family, Geoffery Ridale. Grey, writing in 1649, speaks of the antiquity of the family, and quaintly remarks, "They have been so independent that some have said they kept a boat of their own in the time of the flood, and so were under no obligations to Noah." Sir Nicholas Ridley, who married Mary, daughter of Corwin of Workington, is thought to have been the direct ancestor of Robert Ridley, who married Elizabeth Abridgton in England, and came in the ship *Dorset* to America in 1635.

His son was William Ridley, of Southampton, Virginia; his grandson was William Ridley, of Granville, North Carolina, who married Elizabeth, daughter of Howell Lewis and his wife, Isabella Willis.

Col. Robert Lewis,

Of "Belvoir."

Among the most notable homes of Virginia about the close of the seventeenth century was "Warner Hall," in Gloucester County. The estate was a part of land which had belonged to the Chiskiack Indians, but which was later included in a grant issued to Colonel Augustine Warner.

It was probably given as a dowry to Elizabeth, daughter of Colonel Augustine Warner, who married Colonel John Lewis. The home is supposed to have been built by him, and though at first it may have been a modest structure, later was a very imposing manor-house containing forty rooms.

This home was a centre from which went out to the world men and women who exercised a strong and formative influence upon the communities in which they lived.

OMNE SOLUM FORTI PATRIA EST
LEWIS.

One of these children was Colonel Charles Lewis, to whose family the preceding sketch relates. Another was Colonel Robert Lewis, of "Belvoir," Albemarle County, Virginia, baptized May 4, 1702, who married Jane Meriwether, daughter of Nicholas Meriwether and his wife, Elizabeth Crafford. Elizabeth Crafford was daughter of David Crafford or Crawford, who was born in Scotland.

This Nicholas Meriwether, who died in Goochland County, Virginia, in 1744, was a vestryman of St. Peter's Church, New Kent County, justice of the peace of New Kent, sheriff of the same county, and member of the House of Burgesses.

He was a son of Nicholas Meriwether, who came to America from Wales, and died in Surry County, Virginia, December 19, 1678.

To Colonel Robert Lewis and his wife, Jane Meriwether, were born eleven children:

1. Nicholas, who married Mary Walker, daughter of Dr. Thomas Walker, of Castle Hill, and his wife Mildred Thornton.

2. John, who married Anne ——.

3. William, who married Lucy Meriwether, and had Meriwether Lewis.

4. Jane Meriwether, who married her cousin, John Lewis, son of Colonel Charles Lewis, of "The Byrd."

5. Mary, who married Samuel Cobb, of Louisa County.

6. Mildred, who married Major John Lewis, of Spotsylvania County, son of Zachary Lewis.

7. Isabella, died young.

8. Elizabeth, who married Rev. Robert Barret.

9. Charles, who married Mary ——; they had Howell and Charles Warner.

10. Sarah ——.

11. Robert, who married his cousin, Frances Lewis, daughter of Colonel Charles Lewis, of "The Byrd."

Colonel Robert Lewis died 1757, and his will is recorded in that year.

Nicholas Lewis, son of Colonel Robert Lewis, of "Belvoir," and his wife, Jane Meriwether, was deputy from Albemarle County, September, 1775, for the District of Buckingham, which met to provide for the defence of the district. September 9th he was made captain of the Albemarle Minutemen. He commanded a regiment in the successful expedition in 1776 against the Cherokee Indians, and aside from the qualities which made him a spirited leader of troops, he is said by Jefferson to have been "endeared to all who knew him by his inflexible probity, courteous disposition, benevolent heart, and engaging modesty of manner."

He married Mary Walker, daughter of Dr. Thomas Walker, of "Castle Hill," Albemarle County, and his wife Mildred Thornton. To them were born twelve children, among them—

1. Thomas Walker Lewis, born 1763; died June, 1807; married, 1788, Elizabeth Meriwether.

2. Elizabeth Lewis, born 1769; married, February 28, 1788, William Douglas.

3. Margaret Lewis, born 1785; married Charles Lewis Thomas.

4. Mary Lewis, who married Isaac Miller, of Kentucky.

5. Nicholas Meriwether Lewis, born August 13, 1767; died September 22, 1818. He married his cousin, Mildred Hornsby.

daughter of Joseph Hornsby, of Williamsburg, Virginia, and his wife, Mildred Walker (daughter of Dr. Thomas Walker and his wife, Mildred Thornton). Nicholas Meriwether Lewis and his wife, Mildred Hornsby, moved from Virginia to Kentucky, and made their home near Louisville, at this time only a small settlement. To them were born two children, Joseph, who died young, and Annah Hornsby.

Annah Hornsby Lewis married Hancock Taylor, son of Colonel Richard Taylor, an officer who won distinction in the Revolution, and who was a great-grandson of James Taylor (who came from Carlisle, England, to Virginia about 1635) and his first wife, Frances ———.

On the maternal side, Hancock Taylor was descended from William Brewster and Isaac Allerton, of the *Mayflower*, and from the Lees and Willoughbys of Virginia. He was also a brother of Zachary Taylor, general in the Mexican war, and later President of the United States.

The home of Annah Hornsby Lewis and her husband, Hancock Taylor, was "Springfields," a handsome estate five miles from

Robinson.

ALEXANDER ROBINSON.

Louisville, Kentucky. It was a conspicuous social centre for the gentry of the county, and famed far and wide for its gracious and lavish hospitality. A large retinue of slaves cultivated the fertile acres, served in the house, and attended the masters and mistresses at home and in their travels.

In this home grew to maturity ten children; two only are now living, Robert Hornsby Taylor, of Florida, and Mary Louise Taylor, born May 20, 1824, who married Archibald Magill Robinson, of Louisville (born in Winchester, Virginia, August 23, 1821).

Archibald Magill Robinson is a great-grandson of Alexander Robinson, who settled in Baltimore, Maryland, about 1780.

This Alexander Robinson was descended from the Robinsons of England, barons of Rokeby. This estate, which has been made famous by Sir Walter Scott, still belongs to a member of the family.

On the maternal side, Archibald Magill Robinson is descended from the Goldsboroughs, who were Saxon Thanes, holding their estate, "Goldesborough Chase," near Knaresborough, Yorkshire, prior to the Norman Conquest.

To Mary Louise Taylor and her husband, Archibald Magill Robinson, were born eleven children—

1. Richard Goldsborough, married Laura Pickett Thomas.

2. Lewis Magill.

3. John Hancock, married Frances Lynn Scruggs.

4. Annah Walker, married James Henry Watson.

5. Elizabeth Lee.

6. Robert Lyles.

7. William Brice, married Elizabeth Boyd Rainey.

8. Arthur Edwards.

9. Zachary Taylor, married Susan Luckett.

10. Alexander Meade, married Lillian Hammond.

11. Henry Wood.

Annah Walker Robinson married, October 5, 1870, James Henry Watson, of Mississippi, son of Hon. J. W. C. Watson and his wife, Catharine Davis. Hon. J. W.

C. Watson was member of the Confederate Senate, and a leading jurist of his State. Catharine Davis was the daughter of Staige Davis and his wife, Elizabeth Gardner. (Elizabeth Gardner was the daughter of John and Eliza Gardner, of King and Queen County, Virginia.)

The children of Annah Walker Robinson and her husband, James Henry Watson, are:

Archibald Robinson Watson.

James Henry Watson, Jr., who married June 12, 1900, Katharine Julia Black, a lineal descendant of John Alden, of Plymouth Colony, and his wife, Priscilla Mullens, or Molines.

Katharine Davis Watson.

Elizabeth Lee Watson.

The record contained in this volume closes with the immediate descendants of Colonel George Reade, then follows briefly the lines of Colonel Clement Read, Colonel Charles Lewis, of "The Byrd," and Colonel Robert Lewis, of "Belvoir." It covers a thousand years, and presents a record in which appears some of the most distinguished names of history.

Beginning with the Saxons, it comes down through Norman, English and American families, and, in closing, it would seem not inappropriate to quote the eloquent words of the two latest laureates of the English people—

"Of one-self same stock at first;
Make them again one people—Norman, English,
And English Norman: we should have a
Hand to grasp the world with,
And a foot to stamp it flat."

"We severed have been too long;
But now we have done with a worn-out tale,
The tale of an ancient wrong,
And our friendship shall last long
As love doth last,
And be stronger than death is strong."

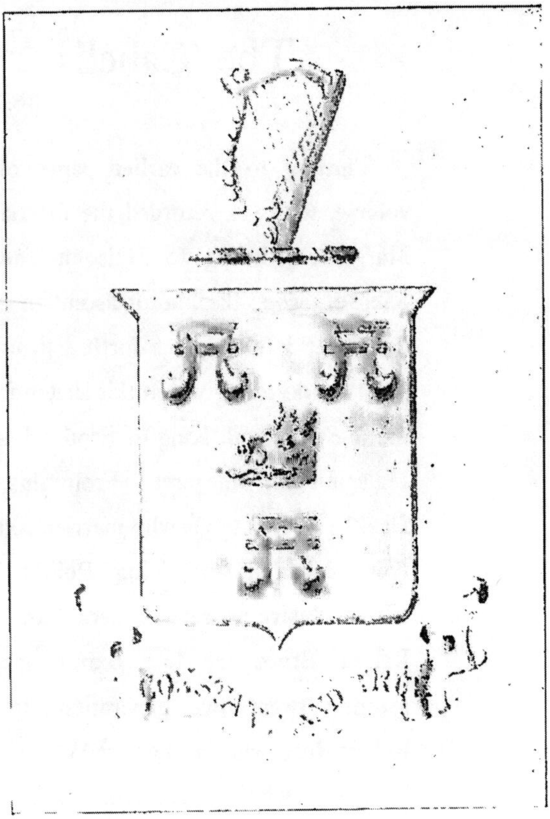

ROSE.

The Cabells.

Turning to the earlier pages of this volume, where is recorded the marriage of Margaret Atheling to Malcolm Canmore, King of Scots, the line of ascent to Alfred the Great is clearly set forth. From that point the descent given in this sketch follows the line of David, King of Scotland, son of Malcolm and Margaret. From this King David (A. D. 1153), who married Maud of Northumberland, to King Robert Bruce First, inclusive, are seven generations. From Robert Bruce the line comes unbroken through twenty-two generations to Rev. Robert Rose, who was born at Wester Alves, Scotland, February 12, 1704, and came to Virginia, 1725. Not only through this line, but four others, was he of royal descent, and in the annals of his house are found the names of the Stewarts, the Campbells, the Earls of Angus, and many others, who were closely associated with the ruling dynasties of Europe.

On the paternal side he was in the fifteenth generation from Hugh Rose of Easter Geddes, who died 1333, and eighth from Hugh Rose, Baron of Kilravock, and his wife, Lady Margaret Seaton.

Lady Margaret was a daughter of Alexander, first Earl of Huntley, and sister of George, the second Earl, who married Princess Joanna, daughter of James the First of Scotland.

Rev. Robert Rose was ordained by the Bishop of London, and after coming to Virginia had charge of St. Annes in Essex, 1726-1747, and of St. Annes in Albemarle, 1747-1751. His strong and forceful personality fitted him well for life in this transition period, and he was not only a leader, a shaper of destinies, but a teacher of the gospel.

In 1735 he discovered the Tye River, a branch of the James, and by order of the Council was granted an immense tract of land on its banks.

He married (second wife) Ann, daughter of Colonel Henry Fitzhugh, of Virginia.

He died in Richmond, 1751, and was buried in old St. John's churchyard, where a monument, erected to his memory by a loving people, is inscribed, "May his posterity emulate his virtues."

Colonel Hugh Rose, son of Rev. Robert Rose and his wife, Ann Fitzhugh, was born September 18, 1743. He was justice of the peace for Amherst County from 1765 to his death, member of the County Committee of 1775-'76, a vestryman of Amherst, and after 1779 of Lexington Parish; was sheriff of his county 1776, colonel of militia, county lieutenant 1780, and member of the House of Delegates 1785-'86.

He married Caroline Matilda Jordan, daughter of Colonel Samuel Jordan.

Judith Scott Rose, a daughter of this union, married Landon Cabell, who was born February 21, 1765, at "Union Hill," Nelson County, Virginia. He was the son of Colonel William Cabell, grandson of Dr. William Cabell, the emigrant, and was a man of rare natural qualities and scholarly attainments. His gracious bearing, brilliant conversational gifts, and charming hospitality made him the centre of a wide circle of admiring friends, and, though he declined the most flattering offers of high political distinction, he served his generation in many positions of trust.

June 1, 1804, he was one of the three commissioners appointed by Governor John Page to supervise the election of presidential electors in Amherst County; was long justice of the peace in Amherst prior to 1808, and from this date for many years a justice in Nelson; of this county he was sheriff, 1815-1816. In 1834 he died at Rose Hall, and here was buried.

Dr. Robert Henry Cabell, son of Landon Cabell and his wife, Judith Scott Rose, was born February 19, 1799, at Montezuma, Nelson County, Virginia. He was educated at William and Mary College, studied medicine at the University of Pennsylvania, and after graduating, 1821, settled in Richmond. Here, in 1823, he married Julia Mayo, daughter of Colonel John Mayo and his wife, Abigale DeHart.

The children of this marriage died in childhood; the death of Mrs. Cabell followed, and in 1860 Dr. Cabell married Mrs. Catherine Eyre Bailey Pelham. She was widow of Charles Pelham, of Pelham Manor, England, a member of the Eyre family of Clifton Castle, County of Galway, Ireland, and descended from a line of ancestors noted for the brilliance of their intellectual gifts. After the civil war, Dr. Cabell moved from Virginia to Baltimore, where he died February, 1876.

Virginia Catherine Cabell, daughter of Dr. Robert Henry Cabell and his second wife, Catherine Eyre Bailey Pelham, married, first, B. Howard Tyson. The children of this marriage were Virginia Cabell Tyson and Juliet Catherine Tyson. She married, second, Charles Herman Ruggles, son of Adjutant-General George D. Ruggles, of the United States Army, retired. The children of this marriage are Anna Christie and Alma Hammond L'Hommedieu Ruggles.

Mrs. Virginia Cabell Ruggles, whose home is in Milwaukee, is a member of the Acorn Club, Philadelphia, Pennsylvania, of the Virginia Colonial Dames, of the Old Dominion Chapter of the Daughters of the American Revolution, the New York Chapter of the Daughters of the Confederacy, is recording secretary of the Wisconsin Chapter of National Daughters of 1812, and Councilor for Wisconsin of the Order of the Crown.

Farnsworth.

Alfred the Great was succeeded by his son Edward "The Elder," whose third wife was Lady Edgiva, daughter of the Saxon Earl Sigelline. Their daughter, Edgiva, married Charles the Third, King of France, who was a descendant of Charlemagne. Louis the Fourth of France, son of Edgiva and Charles the Third, married Lady Gerberga de Saxe, daughter of Henry the First, Emperor of Germany.

From this marriage, through many noble houses, the Counts d'Auvergne and Anjou, Dukes of Bretagne and Normandy, Earls of Richmond and others, the line of descent comes to the Earls of Harcourt, and to Lady Arabella Harcourt, who married Sir John de Digby. He died in 1267, and both were buried at Tilton.

Sir Everard de Digby, M. P., of Drystoke, a great-great-great-grandson of this couple, was High Sheriff of Rutlandshire in 1459. He and his three brothers were slain at Towton, 1461, fighting under the banner of Henry the Sixth. His wife was Anne, daughter of Sir Francis Clarke of Whyssendom, Rutland County.

Their great-great-great-granddaughter, Elizabeth Digby, heiress, born 1584, died 1669, married October 25, 1614, Enoch Lynde of London. He died April 23, 1636.

The ancestral home of the Digby family, Sherborne Castle, is said to be occupied at the present time by Lieutenant-Colonel Edward Henry Trafalgar, tenth Baron Digby.

The genealogy of this distinguished family is preserved at Sherborne Castle in a folio volume of five hundred and eighty-nine vellum leaves, the first one hundred and sixty-five ornamented with the coats-of-arms of the family and its allies, and illuminated in the richest manner.

Simon Lynde, a son of Elizabeth Digby and Enoch Lynde, was born in London June 24, 1624, died November 22, 1687. Like other members of his distinguished family, he was the recipient of many honors, which attested a broad recognition of his worth and station. His presentation to King Charles the First, by his near relative, Baron Digby, of Sherborne, 1618, and First Earl of Bristol 1622, took place not many years before the king's death. After coming to America, he was made Judge of the Superior Court of Judicature at Boston, Massachusetts. He married, in February, 1652, Hannah, daughter of John Newdigate.

Benjamin Lynde, a son of Judge Simon Lynde and Hannah Newdigate, was a Chief Justice of Massachusetts, and his son, Benjamin Lynde, Jr., succeeded to the same office.

Judge Samuel Lynde, a son of the latter, married Mary, daughter of Jarvis Ballard. Mary Lynde, their daughter, married Hon. John Valentine, of Boston, "His Majesty's Crown Advocate-General" of the provinces of Massachusetts, New Hampshire and Rhode Island.

Thomas Valentine (a son of this marriage) married Elizabeth, granddaughter of Sir Charles Hobby, who was knighted by Queen Anne at Windsor Castle July 9, 1705, "for services done the Crown in New England." He was an officer in "The Ancient and Honorable Artillery Company of Boston."

A son of this marriage, Samuel Valentine, married Elizabeth, daughter of Colonel John Jones and his wife, Hannah Simpson.

Their son, Samuel Valentine, Jr., married Mary Fiske, daughter of Captain Richard Fiske, of Framingham, Massachusetts (whose family was descended from Symond Fiske, Lord of the Manor of Stadhaugh, 1399-1422. Many distinguished men of letters have descended from this house). Their daughter, Eliza Fiske Valentine, married Benjamin Stow Farnsworth, of Boston, and had Harriet Eliza Prescott Farnsworth, Henrietta Lynde Farnsworth, founder of "The Order of the Crown," and Mary Susan Valentine Farnsworth, who married William Wirt Smith, of Chicago, and had Edna Valentine Smith.

Some American Descendants of Alfred the Great and Other Sovereigns.

Some American Descendants of Alfred the Great and Other Sovereigns.

In the subjoined list it will be found that each individual is either shown to be descended from a well-known ancestor already traced in this volume, or sufficient data is given to connect him or her with the royal line in some earlier generation. Blank pages are added, that those not entered may include their own lines.

Mrs. Keller Anderson, *née* Jean Millar Robertson, daughter of Hon. James Robertson and his wife, Anne Lewis Dale: great-granddaughter of Frances Taylor and her husband, Rev. Nathaniel Moore; great-great-great-granddaughter of Colonel Charles Lewis, of "The Byrd," and his wife, Mary Howell.

Mr. Claude Desha Anderson, great-great-great-great-grandson of Colonel Charles Lewis, of "The Byrd," and his wife, Mary Howell.

Jean Keller Anderson, great-great-great-great-granddaughter of Colonel Charles Lewis and his wife, Mary Howell.

Mrs. William Blackburn, *née* Isabella Hinton Miller, great-great-great-granddaughter of Colonel Charles Lewis, of "The Byrd," and his wife, Mary Howell.

Mrs. Mary Howard Bruce, *née* Mary Howard, great-great-great-great-great-granddaughter of Elizabeth Reade and her husband, Thomas Chisman.

Mrs. Jonathan Bullock, *née* Emma Westcott, eighth in descent from William Arnold (and his wife, Christian Peake), who came to America in 1636, and was one of the original proprietors of "Providence Plantations." He was twenty-fifth in descent from Hugh Capet, King of France, and his wife Lady Adela of Aquitaine.

Mrs. Frank Percival Bakewell, *née* Mary Melanie Dean; daughter of Carolyn Simpson and Leonard Yancy Dean; granddaughter of Mary Anne Daniel and William Thomas Simpson; great-granddaughter of James Lewis Daniel and Matilda Gauntt: great-great-granddaughter of Elizabeth Lewis and Zadoc Daniel; great-great-great-granddaughter of James Lewis and Susanna Anderson; great-great-great-great-granddaughter of Robert Lewis and Frances Lewis: great-great-great-great-great-granddaughter of Colonel Robert Lewis and Jane Meriwether. Issue: Yancy Dean Bakewell.

Mr. Tilghman Howard Bunch, son of Katharine Henderson and Tilghman Howard Bunch. Katharine Henderson was daughter of Elizabeth Cocke and Joseph Henderson. Elizabeth Cocke was seventh in descent from Colonel Moore Fauntleroy and Mary Hill. Colonel Moore Fauntleroy was twenty-eighth in descent from Alfred the Great.

Mrs. Susanna Digges Cole Chapman, great-great-great-great-great-granddaughter of Sir Dudley Digges and his wife, Lady Mary Kempe.

Mr. Ashton Alexander Chapman, great-great-great-great-great-great-grandson of Sir Dudley Digges and his wife, Lady Mary Kempe.

Mrs. Walter Silas Crane, *née* Anna Augusta Foard, great-great-great-great-granddaughter of Colonel Charles Lewis, of "The Byrd," and his wife, Mary Howell.

Mrs. Thomas Day, *née* Mary Robertson, great-great-great-granddaughter of Colonel Charles Lewis, of "The Byrd," and his wife, Mary Howell.

Miss Mary Louise Day, great-great-great-great-granddaughter of Colonel Charles Lewis, of "The Byrd," and his wife Mary Howell.

Mrs. Leonard Yancey Dean, *née* Carolyn Simpson, daughter of Mary Anne Daniel and William Thomas Simpson; granddaughter of James Lewis Daniel and his wife, Matilda Gauntt; great-granddaughter of Elizabeth Lewis and Zadoc Daniel; great-great-granddaughter of James Lewis and Susanna Anderson: great-great-great-granddaughter of Robert Lewis and his wife, Frances Lewis, who were first cousins, children of Colonel Robert Lewis, of "Belvoir," and Colonel Charles Lewis, of "The Byrd."

Mr. Leonard Yancey Dean, Jr., son of Carolyn Simpson and Leonard Yancey Dean; grandson of Mary Ann Daniel and William Thomas Simpson; great-grandson of James Lewis Daniel and Matilda Gauntt; great-great-grandson of Elizabeth Lewis and Zadoc Daniel; great-great-great-grandson of James Lewis and Susanna Anderson; great-great-great-great-grandson of Robert Lewis and Frances Lewis: great-great-great-great-great-grandson of Colonel Robert Lewis and Jane Meriwether.

Mr. Joseph Judson Dimock, a descendant of Thomas Dimock, who came to America prior to 1635. He is believed to have been a great-grandson of Sir Edward Dymoke, Hereditary Champion of England. This Thomas Dimoke married Ann Hammond, and died in Barnstable, Massachusetts, 1658.

Mrs. Rice Fant, *née* Elizabeth Hull, great-great-great-granddaughter of Colonel Robert Lewis, of "Belvoir," and his wife, Jane Meriwether.

Mrs. John McEwen Foster, *née* Bessie Perkins Bethel, great-great-great-great-granddaughter of Colonel Charles Lewis, of "The Byrd," and his wife, Mary Howell.

Miss Henrietta Lynde Farnsworth, great-great-great-great-great-great-great-granddaughter of Judge Simond Lynde and his wife, Hannah Newdigate. He was a lineal descendant of Alfred the Great.

Mrs. William Farrington, *née* Florence Topp, fifth in descent from Patrick Stuart, Laird, of Ledereich, came to North Carolina in 1739. His wife was Elizabeth Menzies. This Patrick Stuart was twelfth in descent from Robert the Second of Scotland and his wife, Lady Elizabeth Muir.

Mr. Louis Ford Garrard, great-great-grandson of Major James MacGregor, who came from Scotland and changed his name to Thomas MacGehee, will dated 1727. Through this ancestor he is a lineal descendant of King David of Scotland as well as of Alfred the Great.

Miss Isa Gartery Urquhart Glenn, great-great-great-great-great-great-granddaughter of Colonel John Smith, of "Purton," and his wife, Mary Warner.

Mrs. Richard B. Goode, *née* Panthea Burwell Goode, great-great-great-granddaughter of Colonel Clement Read and his wife, Mary Hill.

Rev. Horatio Gates, great-great-great-great-great-great-grandson of Richard Lyman, who came to New England in 1631; a lineal descendant of Alfred the Great and Charlemagne.

Mrs. John A. Halderman, *née* Annie Barbour Doriss, great-granddaughter of Elizabeth Lewis and her husband, Bennett Henderson, great-granddaughter of Mary Randolph (who was granddaughter of William Randolph, of Turkey Island) and her husband, Charles Lewis. This Charles Lewis was son of Colonel Charles Lewis, of "The Byrd," and his wife, Mary Howell.

Miss Annie Halderman, great-great-great-great-granddaughter of Colonel Charles Lewis, of "The Byrd," and his wife, Mary Howell.

Miss Mary Hilliard Hinton, great-great-great-granddaughter of Colonel Charles Lewis, of "The Byrd," and his wife, Mary Howell.

Mrs. William Hull, *née* Mary Lewis, great-great-granddaughter of Colonel Robert Lewis, of "Belvoir," and his wife, Jane Meriwether.

Mrs. Jane Lewis Jackson, great-great-granddaughter of Colonel Robert Lewis, of "Belvoir," and his wife, Jane Meriwether.

Mr. C. W. Kerns, great-great-great-grandson of Colonel Charles Lewis, of "The Byrd," and his wife, Mary Howell.

Mrs. William King, *née* Augusta Clayton, great-great-great-great-granddaughter of Colonel George Reade and his wife, Elizabeth Martian.

Mr. John Calvin Lewis, great-great-great-grandson of Colonel John Lewis and his wife, Frances Fielding.

Mrs. Sumpter de Leon Lowry, *née* William Robards Miller, great-great-great-granddaughter of Colonel Charles Lewis, of "The Byrd," and his wife, Mary Howell.

Mrs. Lemuel Long, *née* Martha Pillow, great-great-great-granddaughter of Colonel Charles Lewis, of "The Byrd," and his wife, Mary Howell.

Mrs. August Mayer, *née* Mattie Robards, great-great-great-granddaughter of Colonel Charles Lewis, of "The Byrd," and his wife, Mary Howell.

Mrs. John D. Martin, *née* Walker Hull, great-great-great-granddaughter of Colonel Robert Lewis, of "Belvoir," and his wife, Jane Meriwether.

Mrs. John Marshall, *née* Rebecca Smith, great-great-great-granddaughter of Mary Warner and her husband, Colonel John Smith, of "Purton."

Dr. Daniel Henry Morgan, great-great-great-great-grandson of Mary Warner and her husband, Colonel John Smith, of "Purton."

Mrs. William Moncure, *née* Belle Chapman, great-great-great-great-great-great-granddaughter of Sir Dudley Digges and his wife, Lady Mary Kempe.

Mrs. Thomas L. Moore, *née* Ethel Bland Dean, daughter of Carolyn Simpson and Leonard Yancey Dean, granddaughter of Mary Ann Daniel and William Thomas Simpson; great-granddaughter of James Lewis Daniel and Matilda Gauntt; great-great-granddaughter of Elizabeth Lewis and Zadoc Daniel; great-great-great-granddaughter of James Lewis and Susanna Anderson; great-great-great-great-granddaughter of Robert Lewis and Francis Lewis, first cousins, and children of Colonel Robert Lewis, of "Belvoir," and Colonel Charles Lewis, of "The Byrd."

Mr. Richard Micou, great-great-great-great-great-grandson of Mildred Reade and her husband, Colonel Philip Rootes, of "Rosewall."

Mrs. William Arthur McNeill, *née* Rebecca (or Reebie) Park Metcalf, granddaughter of Rebecca Cocke and William Park; eighth in descent from Lieutenant-Colonel Richard Cocke; also eighth in descent from Colonel Moore Fauntleroy and Mary Hill (their marriage contract dated 1648). Colonel Moore Fauntleroy was nineteenth in descent from Lady Isobel (or Elizabeth) de Vermandois, who was granddaughter of Henry the First of France (and his wife, Anne of Russia), and eleventh in descent from Charlemagne. Elizabeth de Vermandois was eighth in descent from Alfred the Great.

Mrs. Peter Randolph Neff, *née* Josephine Clark Burnett, great-great-great-great-granddaughter of James Claypoole and his wife, Helen Merces. James Claypoole was son of Sir John Claypoole, of Latham, Lincolnshire, England, who was twenty-third in descent from Alfred the Great.

Mrs. Calvin Perkins, *née* Susie Ashton Chapman, granddaughter of William Cole and his wife, Mary T. Alexander; great-great-great-great-great-great-granddaughter of Sir Dudley Digges and his wife, Lady Mary Kempe. Sir Dudley Digges was a lineal descendant of Alfred the Great.

Mr. Blakeney Perkins, great-great-great-great-great-great-great-grandson of Sir Dudley Digges and his wife, Lady Mary Kempe.

Mr. Ashton Chapman Perkins, great-great-great-great-great-great-great-grandson of Sir Dudley Digges and his wife, Lady Mary Kempe.

Miss Belle Moncure Perkins, great-great-great-great-great-great-great-granddaughter of Sir Dudley Digges and his wife, Lady Mary Kempe.

Mr. Louis Allen Perkins, great-great-great-great-great-great-great-grandson of Sir Dudley Digges and his wife, Lady Mary Kempe.

Mr. William Alexander Perkins, great-great-great-great-great-great-great-grandson of Sir Dudley Digges and his wife, Lady Mary Kempe.

Mrs. Carrie Reade Pickens, great-great-great-granddaughter of Colonel Clement Read and his wife, Mary Hill.

Mr. John Read Pickens, Mr. Henry Berlin Pickens, great-great-great-great-grandsons of Colonel Clement Reade and his wife, Mary Hill.

Mr. Jerome Bonaparte Pillow, great-great-great-grandson of Colonel Charles Lewis, of "The Byrd," and his wife, Mary Howell.

Mrs. James F. Read, *née* Lena Garvin Park, daughter of Rebecca Cocke and William Park; eighth in descent from Lieutenant-Colonel Richard Cocke; also eighth in descent from Colonel Moore Fauntleroy and Mary Hill (their marriage contract dated 1648). Colonel Moore Fauntleroy was nineteenth in descent from Lady Isobel (or Elizabeth) de Vermandois, who was granddaughter of Henry the First of France (and his wife, Anne of Russia), and eleventh in descent from Charlemagne. Elizabeth de Vermandois was eighth in descent from Alfred the Great.

Mr. Samuel Roberson Read, great-great-great-grandson of Colonel Clement Read and his wife, Mary Hill; great-great-great-great-great-grandson of Colonel George Reade and his wife Elizabeth Martian.

Mary Hill Read, great-great-great-great-granddaughter of Colonel Clement Read and his wife, Mary Hill.

Elizabeth Nash Read, great-great-great-great-granddaughter of Colonel Clement Read and his wife, Mary Hill.

Margaret Read, great-great-great-great-granddaughter of Colonel Clement Read and his wife, Mary Hill.

Mr. Martin Sims Read, great-great-great-great-grandson of Colonel Clement Read and his wife, Mary Hill.

Mr. Melancthon C. Read, through Colonel Clement Read and his wife, Mary Hill, great-great-great-great-grandson of Colonel George Reade and his wife, Elizabeth Martian.

Mr. Edward Randolph Read, great-great-grandson of Colonel Clement Read and his wife, Mary Hill.

Mr. Alston Read, great-great-great-grandson of Colonel Clement Read and his wife, Mary Hill.

Mr. William Robards, great-great-great-grandson of Colonel Charles Lewis, of "The Byrd," and his wife, Mary Howell.

Mrs. Charles H. Ruggles, *née* Virginia Cabell, great-great-granddaughter of Rev. Robert Rose, of Scotland, later of Virginia, who was a lineal descendant of King David of Scotland and Alfred the Great.

Mrs. Archibald Magill Robinson, *née* Mary Louise Taylor, great-great-granddaughter of Colonel Robert Lewis, of "Belvoir," and his wife, Jane Meriwether.

Mr. Richard Goldsborough Robinson, great-great-great-grandson of Colonel Robert Lewis and Jane Meriwether.

Mr. John Hancock Robinson, great-great-great-grandson of Colonel Robert Lewis and Jane Meriwether.

Mr. William Bryce Robinson, great-great-great-grandson of Colonel Robert Lewis and Jane Meriwether.

Mr. Zachary Taylor Robinson, great-great-great-grandson of Colonel Robert Lewis and Jane Meriwether.

Mr. Alexander Meade Robinson, great-great-great-grandson of Colonel Robert Lewis and Jane Meriwether.

Mr. Henry Wood Robinson, great-great-great-grandson of Colonel Robert Lewis and Jane Meriwether.

Miss Elizabeth Lee Robinson, great-great-great-granddaughter of Colonel Robert Lewis and Jane Meriwether.

Miss Clarissa Roberts Skinner, daughter of Clarissa R. Bancroft and Ebenezer Roberts, through her father a lineal descendant of Rev. Gershom Buckley and his wife, Sarah Chauncey. Through the Chauncey line a direct descendant of King Henry the First of France and his third wife, Anne of Russia.

Mrs. Edgar P. Sawyer, *née* Mary Eleanor Jewell, great-great-great-great-great-great-granddaughter of Charles Chauncey (who landed at Plymouth in 1638) and his wife, Catharine Eyre. Through these ancestors she is thirty-second in descent from Alfred the Great. (See *Sawyer Jewell Lineage*, by Horatio Gates.)

Mrs. Francis Lee Smith, *née* Sarah Gosnell Vowell, great-great-great-great-granddaughter of Mildred Reade and her husband, Colonel Augustine Warner.

Dr. Charles M. Smith, great-great-great-grandson of Mary Warner and her husband, Colonel John Smith, of "Purton."

Mrs. William Wirt Smith, *née* Mary Susan Valentine Farnsworth, lienal descendant of Alfred the Great through Judge Simond Lynde and his wife, Hannah Newdigate.

Miss Edna Valentine Smith, great-great-great-great-great-great-great-great-granddaughter of Judge Simond Lynde and his wife, Hannah Newdigate.

Miss Margaret Vowell Smith, great-great-great-great-granddaughter of Mary Warner and her husband, Colonel John Smith, of "Purton."

Mrs. William Howard Stovall, *née* Roberta Lewis Franks, granddaughter of Dr. Robert Henry Lewis and his wife, Sarah Ann Minter; great-great-great-granddaughter of Colonel Robert Lewis, of "Belvoir," and his wife, Jane Meriwether.

Mrs. Benjamin S. Story, *née* Jeanie Washington Campbell, daughter of Jane Wray Washington and her husband, Charles Campbell; granddaughter of Needham Langhorne Washington and his wife Sarah Ashton Alexander, claiming royal descent through the first Earl of Stirling.

Mr. Robert Hornsby Taylor, great-great-grandson of Colonel Robert Lewis, of "Belvoir," and his wife Jane Meriwether.

Mrs. Lucius H. Terry, *née* Mary E. Robards, great-great-great-granddaughter of Colonel Charles Lewis, of "The Byrd," and his wife, Mary Howell.

Mr. William Wirt Clayton Torrence, great-great-great-great-great-great-grandson of Colonel George Reade and his wife, Elizabeth Martian.

Miss Patty Thumm, great-great-great-granddaughter of Colonel Robert Lewis, of "Belvoir," and his wife, Jane Meriwether.

Mrs. James Henry Watson, *née* Annah Walker Robinson, daughter of Mary Louise Taylor and her husband, Archibald Magill Robinson: great-great-great-granddaughter of Colonel Robert Lewis, of "Belvoir," and his wife, Jane Meriwether.

Mr. Archibald Robinson Watson, great-great-great-great-grandson of Colonel Robert Lewis and Jane Meriwether.

Mr. James Henry Watson, great-great-great-great-grandson of Colonel Robert Lewis and Jane Meriwether.

Miss Katharine Davis Watson, great-great-great-great-granddaughter of Colonel Robert Lewis and Jane Meriwether.

Miss Elizabeth Lee Watson, great-great-great-great-granddaughter of Colonel Robert Lewis and Jane Meriwether.

Mr. William Ward Wight, great-great-grandson of Rev. Thomas Potwine and his wife, Abigal Mosely, of Windsor, Connecticut. Through these ancestors, also Frances Chister, Jane Fortescue and Sir Richard Champernowne, of Devonshire, England, he is a lineal descendant of Alfred the Great.

Mr. John Nash Wilson, great-great-grandson of Colonel Clement Read and his wife, Mary Hill.

Mrs. W. Blackburn Wilson, *née* Isabella Hinton Miller, great-great-great-granddaughter of Colonel Charles Lewis, of "The Byrd," and his wife, Mary Howell.

Mr. John B. White, great-great-great-great-great-grandson of John Prescott and his wife, Mary Platts. John Prescott was son of Ralfe and Ellen Prescott, Shevington, Parish of Standish, Lancaster, England.

who was a descendant of Alfred the Great through William Fitz Gilbert (Governor of Lancaster Castle, fifth Baron of Kendal) and his wife, Gunred, Countess of Warick, daughter of William de Warrenne and his wife, Elizabeth de Vermandois.

Mr. Pleasants Woodson White, grandson of John Kennon and his wife, Elizabeth Woodson, great-grandson of Elizabeth Lewis and her husband, William Kennon (of Chesterfield), great-great-grandson of Colonel Charles Lewis, of "The Byrd," and his wife, Mary Howell.

Mr. Walker Welford, great-great-great-grandson of Colonel Robert Lewis, of "Belvoir," and his wife, Jane Meriwether.

Mrs. R. W. Williamson, *née* Mary E. White, great-great-great-granddaughter of Colonel Clement Read and his wife, Mary Hill.

Mrs. Sallie Halderman Wilson, great-great-great-great-granddaughter of Colonel Charles Lewis, of "The Byrd," and his wife, Mary Howell.

Dr. James Howell Wilkes, great-great-great-grandson of Colonel Charles Lewis, of "The Byrd," and his wife, Mary Howell.

Lewis *Addendum.*

On page 61, among the children of Colonel Charles Lewis, of "The Byrd," will be found the name of Frances. On page 71, among the children of Colonel Robert Lewis, of "Belvoir," that of Robert (Colonel Robert Lewis, of Louisa County). These two, Robert and Frances Lewis, first cousins, married. Their son, Charles Lewis, born 1773, died December 17, 1819; married, about 1795, Nancy ——.

They moved to Sumner County, Tennessee, where he died, leaving eight children, among them Jane Meriwether, who married K. Harralson, and Dr. Robert Henry Lewis, born May 20, 1811, died January 1, 1871. He married, April 22, 1835, Sarah Ann Minter (daughter of William and Elizabeth Waggoner Minter), who was born December 25, 1815, died April 12, 1878. To them were born, 1. Charles: 2, Joseph: 3. Emily: 4. Robert H.: 5. William Minter: 6. Bailey Peyton; 7. Patterson: 8. Mary Louisa, born April 29, 1848, married, January 22, 1868, Natt Holman; issue, William S., born September 16, 1870 (married Louisa Kaulbach). Anna May, born 1874: Natt, born 1875; Virginia, born 1878 (married Thomas G. Moore); Lou Minter, born 1881; Emma H., born 1885; John T., born 1886.

9. Rosa E., born May 3, 1852, married George D. Perkins: issue, Henry Wright, Robert (died young), George.

10. Roberta H., born October 22, 1854, married June 19, 1873, John N. Hall; issue, Robert Lewis, born 1874: Irene, born 1876: John Nesbit, born 1880: Natt H., born 1884: William Minter, born 1890.

11. Lamira Jane, born July 14, 1846, in East Feliciana Parish, La., where her parents had made their home in 1840. (In 1853 they moved to Texas.) She married, September 25, 1867, Captain Richard Henry Franks (son of John and Mary Ann Ward Franks, of Edgefield District, South Carolina), died near La Grange, Texas, October 9, 1870. Only one child of this marriage reached maturity, Roberta Lewis Franks, born near La Grange, Fayette County, Texas, September 28, 1870, married, July 7, 1891, at Calvary Church, Memphis, Tennessee, William Howard Stovall, of Mississippi (who was born February 20, 1834, son of William Howard and Martha Minter Stovall).

William Howard Stovall, Jr., son of William Howard and Roberta Lewis Franks Stovall, was born at "Prairie Plantation," Coahoma County, Mississippi, February 20, 1895.

